I AM A SCARED WITNESS

Robin (Rochel) Arne

I AM A SCARED WITNESS

AN END OF DAYS UNDERSTANDING

ROBIN ROCHEL ARNE

I am a Scared Witness by Robin (Rochel) Arne
Copyright © 2024 by Robin Arne
All Rights Reserved.
ISBN: 978-1-59755-800-6

Published by: ADVANTAGE BOOKS™
　　　　　　　　Orlando, FL
　　　　　　　　www.advbookstore.com

All Rights Reserved. This book and parts thereof may not be reproduced in any form, stored in a retrieval system or transmitted in any form by any means (electronic, mechanical, photocopy, recording or otherwise) without prior written permission of the author, except as provided by United States of America copyright law.

Scripture taken from the HOLY BIBLE, NEW INTERNATIONAL VERSION®. Copyright© 1973, 1978, 1984 by International Bible Society. Used by permission of Tyndale House Publishing. All rights reserved.

Library of Congress Catalog Number: 20244940030

Name:	Arne, Robin Rochel
Title:	*I am a Scared Witness*
	Robin Rochel Arne
	Advantage Books, 2024
Identifiers:	ISBN Paperback: 978159758006
Subjects:	RELIGION: Christian Life Inspirational
	Religion Biblical Studies - General

First Printing: July 2024
24 25 26 27 28 29 30   10 9 8 7 6 5 4 3 2 1

I am a Scared Witness

Acknowledgements

    Jesus plans my way of being and in doing so I am given insight and honor. I have the value of knowing Him in a personal manner. He is the delight of the spirit and being made in His image grants the heart the ability to place value to Him. God, the one who never fails, is neither a false narrative nor a broken stand of no hope. He is the character needed to offer others a better unity to Him. The way to feed the lost or the one who has not been given light is to supply the written Book of hope to their heart and mind. Leading for the sake of giving others the knowledge God is true is to surpass the understanding that self is better. God is far superior to that of any person, and He offers hope and community to mankind. The delivery of Jesus to the cross benefitted all, not just the weak or the frail. God leads so man finds faith and trust. The idea God is not wholesome is a lie. God is all things right and true for He made the heavens and the earth. The abundant way He designed man specifically is for us to realize He can master the great way of being. The evolved find the way to God by working on the entanglement and desiring Him as their hope. God is ever one to align Himself to that of mankind so he can find support. In Christ man is shown where to grant another the option of fruit-bearing knowledge. The glory of God is well intended. In Him we learn to prosper and how to grant many the saving aptitude of the learned way. Christ is symbolic to the one who believes He is all-knowing. Anyone with a reason to care knows God is perfect in His way of standing. Leading so many find the faith is what characterizes the beauty of the written Scriptures. Knowing God leads the one who takes to heart what is stated in the Book of love. Glory is for all to gift upward to God. Select for yourself a way of trust and embrace truth as a whole. The only one capable of leading mankind into the light is God. He will forever stand as the great Waymaker.

Robin (Rochel) Arne

Foreword

The way to comprehend this material is to believe in the prophesy work of the Lord. The Bible is a solid informative outline of what is to come. Believe the material and learn how to plan for many to find the offered goal. Knowing the One who designed the knowledge is the way to escape the harsh period that is on the horizon. God will soon move and the many left in the wake will have no hope of withstanding the mile high damage that is to come. God has spoken and we need to believe He means what He has declared. It may seem unjust, but man has stepped outside the care and unity God provides. Man has chosen to deliver lies and pain to the doubting generation. Today, little is keeping people standing with character. The value of God has been forgotten. Know where to learn the facts about Christ and be gifted the support to find Him trustworthy. All will attend the Judgment Day and if you have Christ as your Savior, you will not find death. If not, you will be swept away into the dark and suffer for all time. Does this mean there is no hope for the one who has not committed to God and accepted His Son the Living Word? It does if death takes him before a commitment has been stated. One must offer his heart and mind in accord with the One who died on Calvary's cross. Jesus is able to bring one into life eternal where hope resides, and love is ever present. The life of a witness standing for the sake of God will be a committed statement God is who He claims to be. If your background is slim and you have not worked for the unity to Christ, you are not going to find Him supporting you at the time of Judgement. Faith is a gift that needs clarity in order to be a charge for all time. A deathbed sentence can happen, but why place your heart on the pedestal of no intent thinking you can claim God then? You may not be given the opportunity to establish the way to God and you may find death has conquered you with no love or committed value. Satan has always wanted mankind to support him over Jesus. Without realizing it many have believed not choosing is the answer when in truth it is an acceptance of the dark side. To not embrace the One who conquered death is to state you don't believe He is the Risen I Am. There is no better livelihood than knowing Jesus and being tied to Him in support. He is the Lover of mankind. He is just and holy and in Him is the value of us all. Learn the real way to prosper by taking in account the work of God through Calvary and what it meant to suffer and die for man's sinful ways. We are the ones who should perish with no light or saving power, but God chose for us to learn His nature and to aspire to be committed to Him with hope and faith. This is the real Gospel message. God will teach each person willing to learn who He is and how He operates. You need only invest in reading the Bible and what it represents will come before your heart. You will then be able to divulge the truth and to propagate the hope is stands for. Light will ensue and many will learn due to the outreach you present. God works for the offered unity to thrive so believe He never loses the willing. The learning sport of trust is a gift so treasure it and be stable in the way of unity. God will offer the remaining derivative so you will always be claimed by His person. He will not lose your undertaking or work outside your heart and love. He will plant His goal to know Him, and you will find the faith He offers as righteous.

Table of Contents

ACKNOWLEDGEMENTS 5

FOREWORD 7

1: ALONE WITH NO UNDERSTANDING 11

2: SEEKING THE LOVE OF THE SAVIOR 33

3: BELIEF COMES BUT STILL THE PAIN IS HERE 53

4: LIGHT IS DIFFICULT TO FIND 73

5: GLORY IS RISING IN MY HEART 91

6: TO TEACH MANY IS DIFFICULT AND FRIGHTENING 111

AUTHOR BIO 125

Robin (Rochel) Arne

I am a Scared Witness

1

Alone With no Understanding

Today is declared a loss for many who have been swept away to some distant land. We have no understanding as to where the captured ones have flown. Those of us left here to muddle through the chaos are wondering will we ever meet our loved ones again. Darkness is prevalent and only goals of livelihood are being administered. I work as a person on the lookout due to the holding of the Bible I have before me. I am unclear as to the contents or even if I am one worthy to read the contents within. Never have I understood the need to try and gain knowledge as to the reality of Christ. Before, I was happy working and doing my own interpretation of life. God had no influence over me. He was just the idea and not the Creator. I never believed I needed to gift my heart His companionship. I thought I had time to invest in me. Now I wonder why no others around me speak of knowing God. I used to cringe whenever someone talked about my sin nature. It was something I knew I had, but it mattered little. Now I have only myself to listen toward about a witness I know little of. The faith of God to my heart has not gone without my hearing the tug to my person. I just didn't value it. Believing I could conquer my own way forward instead. People here stand without love or hope, but rather self has become the only focus. It isn't clear where the people were placed who no longer reside as they once did, but the same influence is present. Anyone who lived for the hope of mankind has been taken. Jesus is never spoken of, nor is He accepted. Doors are shut to churches and no entry is being given. Bibles are now not available, and I hide mine so as not to be arrested. My grandmother left her witness for me to learn from, but I work from memory now. She is no longer here to ask questions of and no other stands in her place. Preaching is outlawed and no preaching is televised. Snatches of hope are few and far between. Food is tallied and stores make one adhere to the government's standard, which is soon to be an implementation of a mark. I am not comfortable with this new law, but I have no way to fight it. Underground networks are not viewed with support, so no one speaks of the availability to join one. Do I work for the county assessor, or do I leave my profession and try to find unity in some other way? Life goals are not the objective. We must work for the love of the community alone. No more are we given the lead of knowing where to thrive or operate for all doors to individuality are closed. The plan to conquer the people is well underway.

    The door of hope has been closed on me due to the rapture taking shape before I was ready. I never believed the truth of written Scripture. I thought it all just a figment of someone's idea making. I never thought I would have to endure the level of damnation I am experiencing. I have the ability to claim God, but there is the sin in me needing the reassurance I am still one to be claimed. I doubt my own thinking and I do not enjoy looking at where I could have been. It is hard to envision I could have been swept up to Christ in comfort and holy matrimony. It seems unfair for me to complain. I heard about the timing, but failed to press forward in the quest of knowing how to be raptured. I didn't care enough to invite the truth into my heart. It seemed there was just no advantage to bearing witness to the One who made my very self. Now I stand unable to decide where to turn. No one is standing in my corner. God is something I dream about, but I don't find the support I need so no gain is coming forth. Where do I find the unity my grandmother shared? Is it all just a figment of my imagination? Did she really gift me the knowledge as a child? I remember hearing Bible stories about the saving power of the King called Jesus. Does it matter today if I call on Him with hope? Do I even have any within my heart? Are the witnesses of today any better? There are the many who say Christ is here within our midst, but I have no gift of such a sighting. I do not believe He has come to claim me. Thus, I stand waiting and wondering will He truly love me, even though I didn't rush to serve Him. I have the will to call out; yet, I do not. Why am I so indecisive? Where is the root of the goal? Am I alone here with no insight? Does it really achieve anything if I am to offer my heart to His person? Will I know where to find the trust others before me bore? I have never been one to allow another to stand on my behalf. Is it necessary I do now? Will God hear me when I offer myself to Him or is it too late? I am not hard of understanding so the simple profession should come with no alarm, yet I struggle with the idea of knowing God personally. Has something changed on this planet? Is everyone feeling the same as I do? When I was young, I enjoyed Bible camp, and the people were a witness to the saving power of God due to their ability to hear His voice and unite to Him. They would share this and declare God all-knowing so why do I not accept Him as He is, the great One of all? To love the structure of serving a righteous God has never been my objective. I fail to comprehend how to achieve this gift. I look to where my heart leads and I offer it the way I think it should walk. Am I off in this undertaking? Does any of this stand as supportive? Where do I turn for hope? No one today offers any wise stance as far as I have heard. No choice is being given and man now only shares simple gestures of insight as little is recorded to caregiving. Even lame are without a doctor's care, nowadays. Has all of man determined he has the better way? Should I accept defeat and succumb to the level of depravity that is in the streets? Does it matter how I engage? Is there something more to life than bread and water or a good meal of favorite intakes? Care is something of the past. I now have to qualify for basic medical care. Even the weak no longer survive unless somehow a new fellowship is acquired. The learning ability is scarce due to no book material being granted. Doctors perform abortions at a high-risk shelter and no one seems bothered due to it. No longer is there a food host where the broken and the homeless can lean into. Does this mean society on the whole has no more use for the weaker people of the earth? Am I to witness death on a daily basis? Is the value of man now that of how much earnings he can maintain? Bank accounts are forgotten. The digital way is all the craze. They are spouting man now has the ability to share his partnering with those of less means. What about the hard work and the ethics people used to have? Is this the better way? No division between man and money? I have little invested due to spending on a whim on several occasions. I thought there would be ample time to build a nest egg. I never thought I would have to offer it all to the government. I worked many long hours before labor became the only committed thing money could buy. Today man has the support of machines and robots, so little is needed by way of actual ability in the field of ethics and learning. We have been given over to a domain of no education. Where am I to find the quietness of sitting beneath an apple tree? No more is the fruit of this world offered in a free manner. All groves and plantations are managed by the government. Even gardens contained on one's property do not exist. How did this happen so quickly? Was there even a notion of time when man could have had a choice concerning deceptive behavior or did we just evolve over time into depressed witness making?

  Glory is not something I ever believed I needed to have, but I did not invite it to the Living God of all mankind. He to me was merely someone I could think on, but not truly stand with. I determined to stand on my own accord without the need for a solid entity. I never believed in God above that of a simple acknowledgement. All people have at some point related to the One who made them, but were they committed or just thinking about the hope as a boundary to stay clear of. I never thought I could simply take forth the support or even embrace it. I believed I could wait for the day of when I needed something from Him. Far be it for me to underestimate the role of knowing the leader of the earth itself. I am here today, bound by the government and walking in the way of no leading. I don't see where to spend my thought process as I have taken the word of the people around me no other is more valuable than any other. People of the Word used to say Jesus is the way to know freedom, but I felt He would make me worship Him with no intent to serve me. Was this a term I simply relied upon or was it cast to me from another? Belief never carried me to the point of declaring my heart to any being. I looked at the One who made all mankind and felt He was too harsh for me to follow. I did not apply the truth of the Word by investigating who God presented as, so I never learned what His character was truly of. The One who made mankind is thought to be an abundant supplier of hope. Today there is little I ascribe for other than to have unity in some form or another. God is the caregiver or so I thought so why am I not feeling in unity to Him? Does it take a special idea or stand in some way? Is there a written investment needed? Should I have given to the church building project? What mattered to me was stability. I would look to others for my feeling to progress. Someone who made me feel good was the type of interest I had. Many here do not do this for me so I am in need of finding another to garner me forth into hope. God is not who I envisioned as my Savior for I offered myself for many in the way of communication, so I assumed I had many friends. Today most are not even trying to guide any light in my direction. I evaluate the many that are still present before me and find none call my name but rather they try to make me support their idea of a generalized faith. No church building is even offered at this time, so I don't know where to go to find the hope I once heard about. Does God still listen, or has He shut Himself away and now only blesses the ones who turned to Him before the disappearing of so many? What does it mean to offer insight? I look it up online and the only thing presented is to follow the government and get chipped. Does this seem logical to me? …Perhaps. I don't need to live like a lost man. But I don't feel connected to any idea or stand that serves any goal. I enjoy having worked and offered others the ability to thrive, but my own investments are minimal. The faith I used to envision is not something I have been able to provide for myself. Does this mean I am never going to feel right? Will there always be a less than aptitude in my heart? Have the curtain calls all come forth and I missed them? What is the stand of man if not for the sake of another? I used to believe I could conquer any idea and make it be a fulfilling goal, but now I just align to the work before me, and no joy comes into play. It is a strange way to live. What should I be leaning on? There is simply no imagination around the area of my life, and I have heard it is this way everywhere. What is the possible outcome of being in line with the total present system underway? Is there something hidden I am not seeing? Our leader is a man of authority, and he presents as good but, I don't feel connected to his way of leading. Should the stand I take be dismal and dark for there seems no other choice? I have hoped in people and found little to care about. Where is the light I could offer? I used to recognize it, but now it is dim and almost gone. It fades with each attempt at working for the favor of self. Shouldn't this be a sign to my heart? I looked to others for understanding and all I find is loss. Where is the hope I used to see?

My heart is not frigid, but rather just scathing with no knowledge. I don't know where to look for opportunity or standing in the way of insight. What is determined to me is the notion I missed the off chance of knowing where to lay my sorrow. Has there ever been a more depressed era? I think from social studies man has always had the gift of finding trust before him. But today I see no hope of this. People are cruel and intentionally fast to gore their neighbor in the heart. A look to the nourishment of Scripture seems like a way to perhaps have some inkling of how to know something of value, but how should I proceed? Do I need to offer some kind of sacrifice first or is there a step in the middle for this? Should I perform a statement in writing or is there just a note of unity with the first attempt? Where is the desire and ambition to learn? It passed quickly after the people disappeared. I haven't even the nerve to write a passage on a note card as no one has the personality I am looking to share to. What has happened to me? I loved writing to many before the great loss of humanity happened. The value of knowing where to offer love has escaped my heart. I look at the people before me and realize they are the same. No one even offers another the love of a child. People lose interest once one bears it and no offered help comes along. If someone does manage to care for it, laughter is abundant from the shame department. People look at the youth and feel neglect is the answer. Why has this become a way of life? Childlike mannerisms are not accepted, and none can go into marriage for preaching is forbidden and no ceremonies are performed by laymen. It happened so quickly! I was taken by surprise when the day of the event took form. I thought it a mere joke of some kind, but so far none have returned to state what transpired. It was not something I planned for, but recall is faint, and I remember something concerning the end of days. God was supposed to leave some kind of calling I thought. Wasn't there to be advance moments of understanding? Could there have been something and I missed the sign? The entire world was in turmoil and little press aired it, for they believed it better to shield the communities from the harsh reality it presented. Did this make man fall into a trap without realizing it? I wanted peace and harmony and I looked at television as mere entertainment. I didn't look to the news for hope as it all seemed a prepared speech whenever I viewed it. No other option was present as I didn't research reports outside the mainstream media. I thought if I didn't get affected by it, it didn't really matter. Was I wrong in this analogy? It would appear I didn't care enough to learn where the truth lies. If I had, would there have been knowledge come before me? Would I have found the gateway to the learned and would I have been carried away to Christ? I think perhaps with the team of followers He supposedly had, someone would surely have taken it upon themselves to reach me. I never listened though so would it have made any difference? My grandmother tried, but I thought her old and frail with little to offer me. Now I regret not entertaining her more often. She always valued our time together and she never tested me concerning the way I came to her. It was a free request to join her and visit. Nothing like that can be found here, now. Should I surrender and walk into the government's way of practice or is there something more to this Bible? Is there knowledge for me I can't see just yet? Am I weak or just stubborn? Should I step in faith or lean into no offered care. I feel forsaken and alone.

The love of man is not what I need. I can tell I am fading into a loss I can't contain. How is this happening to me? Where did I go wrong? I paid my bills. I gave to the local, community building fund and I even prayed a time or two. I should have listened to the way my grandmother spoke. She was so easy to fellowship in faith with. I don't know how to find the love of God on my own. Shall I invent a way? Is there more than one offering to know Him? I heard to stand on His behalf means one has His love within him. I don't even know what that looks like. I have been trying to discern where to look but to no avail. I haven't lost my footing altogether, but I have little stamina left. Now I need a spiritual awakening, but where do I find it? Is there some course of study I could learn? Even if it did exist, the government wouldn't allow me to review its material. Today all the workings of truth are gone. We imagine where to learn and that is to suffice us with a goal. I don't like not hearing the way to stand. On occasion, I invested in a trial of gain by admitting I wasn't my all in all. I never believed it though, so I didn't gain the delivery I needed. I invent what I like and look to it as value but now it is all shame and lengthy lectures of no truth. How do I know this? I can't find the unity I have heard exists. My grandmother told me she knew who her Savior was and how to gain His partnering. But I have forgotten the basics of what she quoted me. Does any other feel as I do? No one speaks of this for fear of being jailed and called to testify against the high court of a judge who has no righteous lifestyle. The plan for man has changed from individuality to that of a union in name only. The weak are forgotten and those with ailments have no advancement. A shelter doesn't exist for learning support. No doors are open for gain to be a witness. I haven't even seen a person bow his head for the entry to a room. Where women used to be catered to, and now only the brutish break forth; it is not a gentle time.

    I travel for work not enjoyment. Long gone are the trips of fun and exploration. There is no hope, for the majority have the goal of making money over that of true nourishment to the heart. No one likes to deem favor for the goal of growing in faith. It is merely for the better of oneself people exchange a workstation for the next bounty of favor. The meaning of knowing where to guide has been forgotten. There are no mentors or people of leading. Everyone is out for his own value not that of another. No promotions happen due to any knowledge being given so others advance. If a person decides to acclimate to the routine of simple labor, they are held in contempt. To strive for the sake of money is the only way to achieve recognition. Even then, no value is witnessed. Should I be the one to make a change and stand for unity? Do I dare offer the work of my fruit so another can claim hope? Would this start a chain reaction and bring mankind back into the game of faith? I doubt I could muster enough aid to bring anyone forward, for I too, am not gaining in structured unity. It is not easy to claim no hope. It makes one lost and without insight. The value of God is for all mankind to inherit or, so I was told. Does it even matter I ponder these things? Today there is only strife and no logical attending of the spirit. It is just existence with no honor. I look at my dire circumstance and believe why would God do this to mankind? Does He not love all of man? I thought He did. I don't think I have enough knowledge to support this vision. What would it mean if I did? Would I then have the ability to glide forward and share the love of Him? Is the unity real and I just needed to invite His directive into my heart? Is salvation even a thing? Grandma said it was. In God was supposed to be the way to find freedom. Can it be this easy as just a free word to God? Would He even listen?

    I aim to please the One who gifts me hope, but I don't know where to find Him. The unity of knowing when to vest forward and where to find this gift is a strange feeling. I haven't understood where to turn in the past nor have I hoped to find the answer. I existed to please my own heart, not understanding it was in need of fruit. How do I perfect such a feat where no unity is gifted? God is perfect and just but why hasn't He made me one of His? Am I the one to make the first move? Should I offer myself to Him out of respect and honor? Does He need me to say the words? Should I commit to Him with abandonment or is there another way? It seems too hard of a partnering in where I have to succumb to Him for a better way. Perhaps, I have not heard His voice as some spoke of in the former life I knew. To value the Risen One of character is what people claimed. How am I to know where to find this support? Is there enough of Him to support my claim of faith or have all the people before me used up the gift? How vast is His power? Even now I have no expectation of trust due to none being in-house any longer. I value the One who made mankind, but I never thought I had a need for His way of being. What would it look like if I now ask for the invitation to His person? Does He invest under the guise of no shouldering? Do I need to truly believe or is it enough to just simply say the words without the measure of trust within them? It would seem to me He is all-knowing, so even if I did say something to the nature of surrender wouldn't He just laugh? Do I truly want Him over the governing body I see now? There is ample love taking, but no soul invested care and I preferred it the way it was before the people went missing. So, what am I to incorporate with my thinking now? Shouldn't there be a manual or printed article or something?

Would it have made a difference to me if I read such a thing? I never thought I would be in this type of situation. Dark thoughts come readily and no other shares light in front of me. It would seem unusual to me now. Has the ship sailed without my favor upon it? Would God grant me the way of many just to lead me into a harbor of faint knowledge? Is He that type of being? I think God knows my thoughts so why doesn't He offer me the plan of His witness?

God is unique to my thought process. In His support others have known how to offer their spirit. This I learned and remember from verses my grandmother shared, but they don't impact me as they did her. Why did she believe so richly in where I only think and ponder? Was there a magical inside witness I never received? Was I supposed to hear something more than I did? Why am I so uninvolved with the true nature of the One of greatness? I have little before me I enjoy. I used to make things for fun and for the love of the experience. Today my labor is for the gain of wealth nothing more. It speaks of no true longing just a way to have money to operate. Soon something will point to the way I have chosen but will it be the way to thrive? I have the vested heart of God due to knowing He made man in His image, but this only confuses me. Were we to worship Him on bended knee all day or did our actions speak to Him with favor? I never knew I was without a love detail until the disappearance of the many happened. That is when my heart felt a tinge of remorse even though I never felt the Holy Spirit, I read of Him. Simple words from poetic style writings prospered me. It was all I needed to be present with the world. I enjoy dining in now rather than investing in the limelight of table witnessing at a restaurant. No one offers a plan to eat with another. There is no need or draw. What claimed me to ask what happened in the heart I do not understand, but I know there is a distinct change. I have given to the majority and found life is not the same in this way. I used to plan for an outing, and I would look for social events to better my outlook to another. Today I don't desire to congregate with others. The work of it is too much of a strain. Why would this be? I know there is a difference in how people are gifted. Some enjoyed meeting with many but others only a few. Now no one wants to attend to something other than their own standing. Should this send a red flag my way? Does it have significance? Am I in a battle I can't win or unite with? Do others think the same or are they happy being robots in life? The luxury of having a unity to a partner has been taken away. People aren't partners with one another any longer. They simply couple then forget the experience. Why would it matter to have a long-standing relationship in where another is important to you? I used to have friends I dated but not for the fact of marriage; yet, this somehow is not the same as it was. There was a connection even if I didn't want there to be.

Embarrassment would come into play after the fact but now there is no shame or regret. Just a fact of it happening, then a forgotten undertaking it becomes. How do I accept this as good? Should I review this stand and change my way of thinking? Am I lost in thinking there is more to a relational experience than the physical side? Where would I learn any knowledge concerning this idea? Do others look at this too or am I the only one left to contemplate mankind's existence?

I haven't understood the Glory on high, nor have I ever applied it. I thought I would have to be submitting to God all day without having my own favor upon me. Did I lose something in the way of support due to this idea? Am I ever in the way of faith or have I only just envisioned a stand without actually having one? Did I believe but not in the way others have who knew God? What does this even look like? Should I wear some kind of offered redemption quality or did another make this plea? Did I hear something at one time concerning God Himself being the gift to mankind? Did salvation come into play in some form or another? Have I been under the influence of no actual stand where man was my only hope? Do I need to have more than an idea of hope rather one of unity instead? How does the mind capture the One who he has never seen? Is there a way to believe without declaring something in a righteous way or is the saving power from the One of good influence known as Christ the King? The value of knowing where to find the unity is a hope I engage toward, yet I have only just understood I am at fault in this loss. I never thought I would have to endure such a difficult time. Man is not a witness to each other. He now passes on the gauntlet only to claim the spirit of knowing his own unity. I don't find favor from any other person, so I know something has changed. How to justify what has happened is a difficult thing to assume. I am near to death's door; in I have no goal before me I enjoy. Work is a mere idea of making wealth; yet, the many that flourish are few and far between. The governing body of people have taken our earnings and spread them to the air of the sky. Meaning, no one has capital to claim on his behalf. It must all go to the corporate of the governing body. To have a home is long forgotten. We now share our property with those in need whether they apply themselves or not. It is not the world of corporate ideas and man has ingenuity but rather there is little in the way of inspiration. All the artwork of prior knowledge is now simply a blank wall of color loss. No one paints for the pleasure of sharing an expressive memento nor is there any book writing. All we learn by is the prepared statement from the governing body without reporting on merit. No one can investigate, or build a different accounting for fear of being hanged or jailed for speaking out in a different manner. It has taken only a few items of loss for people to lose the hope of being individualized. It came in a quick manner, right as the people who vanished. How can this be right or good? Man not having any insight from his own thought process. Where am I to find the support I used to have? Can I even expect a learning aptitude since man no longer embraces knowledge but rather supports the governing way of living? Am I the only being on this planet thinking this way? Have I no favor from anyone? Would I ever have the hope I once knew? Should I just step back into the formation of work and no life hope or fanciful idea making? Does it mean I have no regard for another but only a slim focus to survive? Where will I learn and gain in the manner of structured integrity? Should I cave and stop considering such things? Would I be better off not to question the alternative to what is taking place around me?

  The goal of me is self today in where all I love is forsaken. My feelings of inadequacy are strong and met with doubt. My yearning never ceases. My care is slim and without knowledge of what value remains within me. Little by little I care less and all the hope residing in the goals of today are minimal. Man has no hope outside himself. Is this all there is to life? Shall I forever have a loss in understanding where no unity is found?"God above, if you hear me, say something to my spirit."Where is the love I heard spoken of? Where is the value to mankind if not from your hand? All the days of being in a stand of little has cost me my support system. I used to be one of intent with purpose to my day. Now I have only the vast questioning of what to find for my heart to feel alive. Once again, I am in need of knowing where to turn. The perfect, true hope I had is no more. Even before the night of the disappearance I had some idea of what made me happy. Though it may have been false, it felt good to me but now I have nothing within me but a blank stand of loss. Where does one apply to find the root of happiness? Are the people here just working as I do with no favor or maintenance of group love? All the doubting makes me fear and I have no longevity to survive. Should I take my self into the abyss of no more? Will that make me reside in some form of hope or is there nothing after this life? I have the hope of finding a better intake but where do I turn for the unity? Should I be taking tablets of medication for some way to feel? Is there anything outside dark thoughts and impressions anymore? All I find is loss. Everywhere I look no hope is gifted. People are all complaining and in need of some kind of benefit. The government medicates any who come for this relief. Is that what makes one feel again? Is the high of a drug all there is to this life eternal? I have thought for myself it can't be good to intake substance abuse. I have never felt as though it would gain me. None I know who do indulge have ever claimed freedom. Why should I accept defeat where no insight is standing? But how do I expand my wealth of the heart? My grandmother was a respective, prayer warrior, and she often told me she hoped I would be also. I don't even know where to begin. Do I have to kneel or bend the knee and bow my head for it to make a difference? Are there rules to follow and is there a guide to the witness? I should have listened more, but I was too busy believing I was complete on my own. I never felt I wasn't in control, so why bother to change? Would I now reside in heaven if I had?

    The river of silence builds, and I find no comfort from it. Man is not wise in his own understanding in that only by the witness of Him does one build. How can this be if still I have no faith? Man is supposed to be above all else but to me he is weak and unworthy to be praised. The government says to support us all as our own unique being of sight, but where is the truth in this? Man alone makes little corresponding way of unity. The tie he holds to himself is not worthy of unity for each person bears his own cross and has no ability to save another. The witness of man is that of a harsh leader I can't abide to. The way I have stayed outside the draw of him has been to not apply my heart in his direct path of counsel. Why do I resist when so many have not? Is it due to the love of something I don't comprehend? Am I at work in the way of my own entertainment without truly knowing my own agenda? Is there a pull on my mind outside the character of him? I think I have been spared the way of loss simply due to not engaging in his practice of slave witness making. I don't bow down to him at this time for I feel a restrictive nature not to do so. I can't explain why it happens, but it is real, and intent is withdrawn. I do know I can't continue for much longer as it has become the way of him to demand all men to bow to his image and profess him god. I think there is more to this than meets the mind. I feel like I stand on my own merit in that I have not grown in favor of such a man. But is it due to some other acting on my behalf? Is the battle for me just beginning? Is the playwright underway where I have to accept him as my lord? I do not see him as such. He is weak in my estimation though he professes peace and harmony he does not reflect it. Food is even withheld when one goes out against him. He only invites the weakest of many to his party stand of sex driven orgies and lax moral code. How do I gain outside his character when he operates as the great one to mankind? I do not see him as this, but others do. Some have fallen over face down in his presence which seems strange to me. I know the saving witness is a facade due to the many that have fallen and not regained life. He is death to my heart, and I see him as a man of no guiding light. But what am I to do now the rule has come forth where man must accept him as his leader? I have little to offer for my defense other than the notion he is a fraud.

To find the love of something worthwhile is hard to invest in due to there being no value to anything I have today. I enjoyed being a person who shopped and placed money into clothing and such foolishness. Now all I see is empty closet space. We are to wear the same clothes day in and day out. All uniforms and dire coloring, no brightness is ever awarded due to the government declaring bright hues are not becoming to the body. Such a descriptive way no longer seems highly desired, but I feel like a doormat with no foundation or value. I loved having things of beauty but now we must refrain from the luxury of both color and the beauty of the rare diamond. No more are jeweled hands or the waist belts as they emphasize the need to be more upright. We are taught to be nondescript with no adornments of any kind. I value some of the wealth in my account, but I can't apply it in the way I would like, so what value does it have? The governing body makes the decision for me as to where my money goes. And I can't find the joy in this as they state it is present, but in truth it only makes me want to learn something for myself and not share it. I used to read story books and envision the many fields of opportunity, but today there are only news ports with outlets of government material, nothing with character or idea making. It is a designed element no longer valued. I have little to no sunlight in my office cube and at home I must pull the drapes as it is mandated I do so. I look at the cloud covering and miss the cool remembrance of rain and snow. It use to mean a change in the weather was an indicator of new life, but now we must call it climate change and fear it. I do not see the harm in a good thunderstorm. Man can endure the rare lightning strike when he is sheltered inside but he could see out the window in the past. Today no one is permitted to look out of doors or breathe in the fresh air. They insist it is for our own good, but I know this makes no sense. Who is the one to dictate all these mandates…but none other than the governing body of today? How this happened only God can tell me for I did not strive for such a way. I did not protest against it, but I thought others would defend our right to bear arms and fight for the better of us all. No one can carry a weapon in sight of the armed facilitator. He will strike anyone who dares to try to stand against the great leadership we have in play. Guns were outlawed and man failed to fight for the right to lead. We caved and came to a stand of no implementation for the right to defend our own way of living. America has no stand either for she lost the right to work on her own accord by signing away her livelihood to the other countries that had little to offer. Why did this happen? Should we now try to take back this homeland? Would there be anyone willing to stand up for the sake of others? I see no counterpart willing to defend the right to have a life of full hope. So what am I to do? Where am I to incorporate the unity? Should I reach out and ask others how they feel about this, or will it mean imprisonment in the quickest of forms?

    I have the hope man will change and once more value his neighbor, but I don't know how to invest in this change. The one who steps out of line finds the strap of the whip against him. Jail terms are prominent, and no one ever sees a jailed person return to his training facility. I have only my own suspicion as to where they end up, but who am I to say for sure? I think the manner of them is loss and no return of the primary happens. The labor of work is all there is to assume a job well done but even this is only fleeting. Many have asked to just lie in the muddle of no hope and have taken to the idea of eating to fulfill their faith. There are rations so indulging comes at a price. To eat your food quickly means no fulfillment later in the week, so it is hard to stay connected to even this small entity. The level of rations is for the one who does the most for the community, not that of self. Sharing your labor so others have the benefit of the good you do is a difficult dream to uphold. I believe I am not the only one who feels this way; however, no one mentions this for fear of facing charges of hate. Hate speech is prominent and it takes very little to have an implementation of this charge against you. I have found talking little is the best way to stay clear of this charge. To not speak has cost me the voice I once knew, and I now have only my thoughts. I have to keep silent in that my opinion is not what the order demands. I have no knowledge of what many are witnessing or learning due to this restraint. Sharing the value of love is not even something contemplated. Man has to have the way of a present lean that speaks only of the high master, or he is banished to a life of hard labor in a training camp. No people I know have ever returned who dared to stand against the labor contract. They have never been heard from or seen, so I doubt they even exist now. Should I be grateful for the level of life I do have or is this hell on earth? Did I lose the guiding light by merely ignoring the way to thrive in God? Was it even something I could have cared to do? I am without the insight, so how can I expect to learn? Should I cry out to the One who made mankind? Did He forget those who were not taken in the disappearance? Are we to live in eternal damnation as a result?

God is the one who made heaven and earth, or so I was convinced by the way my grandmother spoke. She made me believe I was valued by the One who made all things right and good. I have no knowledge of whether this makes me a committed being of insight or just simply one who heard but did not apply the truth. God has never been my focal point. I believed if He cared He would work out the details of my salvation and I would have the knowing way of faith within. I never thought I had to apply my own faith to Him. Is this the difference I needed to have been selected for eternal gain? The way to acknowledge God is simply not spoken of here. We must stay silent; if we press the issue we are punished and made to think we are just conceited with no hope of care. God should have shown me a better way. What it would have taken I do not know but being in this time frame has made me think I should have been more inclined to learn about Him. I enjoy a gift of hope but there is none to be had. Even the slim chance of it has faded in where no other thinks as I do that I am aware of. All the way of many is to stand for the government and to expect it to perform for the good of mankind but I don't see this taking form. The goal today is to offer aid in the way of simple knowledge so others have the ability to guide in the manner of self. We are taught to offer no reward for being informed, but to claim the knowledge and secure it away from anyone seeking to learn from our hand of instruction. How can man operate in this manner? Won't society as a whole fail? I believe no benefit means to allow a loss to ensue rather than for gain to happen, but I am taught this is not true. Shall I prove my stand worthy of help or am I not ready to justify my own thinking? It would mean a loss in revenue and a charge applied to my account. What should I invest my knowledge toward? What matters most to the ones in my area of this region? Should I believe I am within my rights to offer another a better stand? Would it mean no future for me as an operator here at my employment facility? Would I have to endure hard labor for the rest of my days? The fire within is faded and I look around and find no joy. No output of value is ever heard, and this is intensified by no insight or leading. The goal to survive isn't even something I aim for. Suicide is prevalent and no one speaks to the average loss. The mere mention of it causes one to be given a reprimand; so I choose to remain silent on the subject. I have family missing and I claim silence in this regard also. To speak of the disappearances, one finds themselves hoisted away and enslaved for speaking what might have happened being that of God given. The many who have tried to tell of the rapture from Scripture have been rounded up and thrown into the furnace of hate. Do they ever find a way home?

I am a Scared Witness

Not that I know of…for none have contacted me. I accept I may have taken too long to offer my heart to the One of care, but does this mean it can't happen now? Should I read Scripture and learn the message of unity or is there no point to the unity? God cared enough to send His Son to the cross for me to be given life eternal, but where is the proof? I am in this Godforsaken time frame with no leading or instruction. Would a God of love fail mankind in such a way or was it my own refusal that put me here? Should I have loved Him enough to declare Him righteous and holy? Would the commitment have been the way to Him? What matters is where I end up upon death and this seems like I am there already. These days are long and hard to complete. Many leave work before the end of day and take a loss in the bank so they can invite a party of one to their living quarters. To have to share a place with many is difficult and no privacy is in play. I long for a hot bath but water is now tallied, and we aren't allowed to have but one shower a week. This means the body decays between washings. No one has the account of a full weeks pay as the witness is always saying there is not enough work being recorded though all strive to complete the projects before them. I don't believe we make a shortfall. I am led away from the possibility of having a car or home due to the inapt way of maintaining them. No gardeners are permitted, and no mechanical motors are given. We are to accomplish weed control with spray and it is deadly to the lungs and heart. We have seen many fail to live due to the role of using the chemicals provided by the same people who offer us goal setting. Should I simply believe this is all there is to life or am I to apply the Word of the Book of hope and gain some insight? Will it make a difference to me if I do?

    God has not shown me who He is, but I believe I can find a better thought process if I operate in name to His counsel. Does this mean I need to apply the work of my hands to His person, or do I accept defeat on a whole? Should I believe He cares for my days and He is vested within me? Is there support from on high and I just can't see it? To know the One of courage is a vast dream I hold on to. I haven't lost all knowledge, as I remember my own thought process. Today I looked at the moon and understood it was made in a perfect way. Did God desire for me to recognize Him in this or did my own imagination play a role? Should I think more on this matter or am I failing to author the true knowledge if I do? God created all things right said my grandmother. In her idea of God beauty was presented. I never held fast to the idea He loved all mankind. Even the slave or the murdering villain He was said to care for. How can such a God allow for this world to exist? The loss felt is so strong. Where is the light now? Did God fade away and lose His own value? Is He waiting for the perfect time to attack and kill what remains of mankind? Am I awake or even here? Not knowing where to turn is a stand of no merit.

God is perfect my grandmother would say so why is man in need of Him? Couldn't He have offered a way for man to have unity without the sacrifice of his own heart? Does it even compute to live without your own understanding or am I out of touch with the way it all comes together? God should show me where to go and how to operate and then allow for me to do what I choose. Even this would be courage today. Is the way of trust that of blind knowledge or is the Bible a record of what to do and how to find favor? Should I accept I am without the ability to gain due to no knowing aptitude and lead? Did God forget I was here? Should I bow in respect; yet, not truly invite Him within me? Would this be an answer? I don't know what the best decision is. God has never offered to me a reason to stand on His behalf. All my invested care went unnoticed, so I feel He didn't redeem me as I wasn't good enough. Is this a lie or am I finding a breakthrough in this meeting of my mind? Going into the market today meant I had to pay with my outstretched card, but this is soon to become a form of payment directly from my hand or forehead. I am not sure I like the idea and I have contemplated not accepting the mark due to fear and an unsettled spirit. God did not show me the true nature of this, but I don't enjoy the idea of it. Would grandmother have known what this meant? Maybe she told me, and I didn't pay attention to her wise words. I should have talked with her more. She always had an answer to my questions concerning Jesus and the end of days. She would support my quiet thoughts and let me think on my own understanding, but if she forced me to listen maybe I would have chosen her path. Does it even work in such a manner? Can anyone be a spokesperson for God or do the networks have to represent Him? I knew of televised recordings from before where man could learn how to hear a message from God, but was it for real? Some people claimed to have been reborn, but how did this happen? A child cannot come forth then grow and return to the womb. A mother would die, so I am missing some form of knowledge in this area of learning. Would I understand the Scriptures, if I read them? Do I need to accept Jesus before I can claim the knowledge? Is there some guide I can find? Would God not offer to me a plan and a hope so I can stand in awe of Him? Is He shy or quiet not really a warrior? I am not use to the idea He is weak for what kind of God would He make if he were? Little by little I have thought of who stood on behalf of God before the people went missing and none of them remain but for a few. I assume they did not believe as they stated for no one with the light of God remains. A day ago, I favored a man who had a simple gesture in my direction. I knew he was listening to my call in the call room, but I didn't have the way about me to lean into his warmth. It was a fleeting moment which I let pass by and now no recognition is taking shape. He doesn't even look in my direction now, so I missed the opportunity to meet him and learn something of value. Many find the love of a caress all they hope for, but I know it is shallow with no prosperity to it. The married couples had to separate, and they too now just dally with flirtations. Should this be the standard of matrimony? To me it is a weak manner. I used to envy married couples who were in love. They were visible before the disappearance, but no more. The slight indulgence leads nowhere so why risk the infectious diseases circulating the globe? I believe in love but no other has made an advance to me that seemed right or good. I value the way it was before when men and women had relationship goals with more than just a one-night stand with no meaning. Far be it now for this to happen. Male coupling happens as well as lesbian affairs and this is all the rage. To me it is out of the way of goodness and purity. I can't express this knowledge, as I will be considered operating in the hate realm, so I remain silent. Better was the time of heterosexual gain than today's manifestation of sin. I see man needs a better way, but how to appoint this to others? I can't even realize why I understand it.

May I one day understand the vitality I used to have? Will there be again a reconning in where man finds the faith he used to know? Is the ballet box open to more hope? Should I believe I am here for a purpose or simply a stand in unity? Will I know freedom for my own value or am I now forever alone with no insight? Doing the reading of Scripture is said to align with God but what if I never have the energy to do this? Should I simply accept defeat and walk on in the darkness? Is it a goal to believe or is it some kind of manner yet not known? Do all the many that pushed forth into the heart of the One who made them have the goal they sought? Did they meet their Maker in peace? Is heaven real or just a myth? Should I admit I know little to nothing when it comes to Jesus? Does He care I suffer? Is He watching me, and I don't see Him for the God of hope He is written about? I should have valued Him before the great loss ensued, for it was a simple thing then to state God was your Savior. Today I must keep quiet about my thought process and soon even that will be taken from me. Implants are being implemented and people are forced to embrace them for the sake of the community. I don't feel subject to love when I ponder how they work. Will I be changed for all time due to their programming? Is it even safe to do? I haven't seen another with the bond to God once the implant has been administered. People seem robotic rather than complete and in good standing. Freedom isn't something they represent but rather that of a slave with no idea making of their own. The belief of a wise individual is something I long to witness. When man determined to stand outside the way of hope many found it prosperous to their idea of unity, but I was not enthralled. I desired a path of individualism. I like to see other's ideas be brought to life and today this doesn't happen. The way I lead is with my own thought process but never with action for fear of being tortured and whipped. The governing body stands proud, and no one is allowed to claim a different idea as it goes against the belief of one power overall. Nations all embellish in unity as one body governed by one man. He is a tyrant and not wholesome. He preaches man must be silent with no viewpoint. He alone is the one to say how man is to live and his way is evil in my estimation. To perfect mankind is not possible for all people have different viewpoints when allowed to express them. Leading ended and now the police stand as guard at all the political events. We have no hope of seeing a movie or a play as it is said this is for the lame and the weak. I never thought this the case when I had the freedom to venture to such a place.

Tonight, will be no different in I will abstain from going forth to the market. It is such an endeavor and so hard that it barely seems worth it. Clothing is all the same colorless and nondescript. I don't like the style of the dress making and men have to wear sleeves, or they are committed to the hard labor camps. Is this to be our only way of being from here forward? Am I never to see a bright light in my dress appearance? Has the beauty all been removed? Even cars all look alike. No more sports cars, as they are for the wealthy only. The people who have stood for the new way of being are tied to government. No one with a medium income has the ability to build a new formula of any kind. The mere wage received is only a minimal way to exist. I like to have chocolate, but that too is gone from the shelves. Where am I to find an expression of hope, if the food isn't even worth eating? Meat has been banned so no flesh is consumed. Why did this take place? Man has been instructed to eat only vegetables and no fruit either. Where did the idea health markets needed to be only of a vitamin of no intake for the taste buds to enjoy. Yes, vegetables can have flavor but without seasoning and refreshing salt they are not as appetizing as they once were. People must wear an apron of one endowment with no character for the curve of the body. No, I don't begrudge a stand for individualism. I would be without feeling if all I liked was one look and no value in beauty. Man used to be given samples to choose from but even that went away. Now we must accept what the governing body makes us prepare. The seamstress has no gift to share, or she is put in chains. Does it really matter how straight you walk if you have no hope to live for?

My hope does not come due to no insight or gain from another. Did I value mankind before God? Did it make a difference in my stance? Should I push now to learn and gain in the way of knowledge or is it too late? God is the one I believe holds the way to life eternal. I am not in need of unity to mankind for it is not the way to prosperity. Looking to care for another now means being kept in isolation due to it being forbidden and against the law of the governing body. No guns are present but in the hands of the people with power and they press into man with no hope. I value the option of hearing Scripture, but where do I go to learn it? The Word of God is nowhere to be found except hidden in some hollow shelter. The false technology is everywhere, and we aren't allowed to read so how can I find the necessary way to learn? Should I make my own understanding? Is this how one exudes love forward? I tell myself I knew where to find support, but it is merely a negative thought process today. The unity of faith is not for all to gain as not everyone is trying to invest in something outside the governed way. I like to be different and on my own merit, but that even seems false. How shall I lean into something I know little of? Is the value of my idea making standing in the shadow of remembrance? Did I ever hear the truth or just acquire some unity with no backbone to it? Are there any like me who invent ideas but do not share them with others? Where would one look for this knowledge? Should I offer my thoughts to those in my circle of work? Would they even care if I did? To believe in the One who made you is not something taught these hours in time. Glory is not for man. It is merely put toward the one who leads the people. He never passes legislation to offer us time for ourselves. We must face hard times if we ask for such a pass. To entertain in the way of faith one is fed to the wolf of doubt in that no opportunity is granted. I look to the people in where I have placed my growth and find little comfort from them. The sergeants are not valued but served due to the threat of death. Is this how we are to advance? I see no way for it to happen but only a significant loss of support. I invest where I am welcomed which is only at work with the stand of more for the governing body, not myself. I have listened to the many that failed due to exhaustion and have the idea working for another brings despair. Shall I have no offered collateral or is this what a witness of labor looks like? I used to build in the bank so I could thrive with retail goods, but now I am not given even a penny for my own taking. To me this qualifies as pure indignity with no heart or emotion. I have value to offer, but why apply when all I bring forth leaves my hand? I don't entertain any offers of advancement, as it means I must work longer hours with no more income. Just to say I have a title means little to the expectation of unity. Where is this to go from here? I have no time to tally forth the better of a situation due to no hope or insight. What is the final verdict? Love is gone and no hope is present. This is death but with air to the lungs.

My own idea of being a stand of hope was to offer another the option of being partnered to me in the sales field. I did telemarketing and supported many with this option. I know it meant offering my friends and family on the platter of a sales revenue for my own gain. But it served them by being a product they could use for the goal of self. Now there is only the hope of a return in where all the marketing is for the governing body. Why would I attempt to support the people who make me poor rather than my own self pocketing? I have stood for the cause and found it lacking. I enjoy being given the ability to attend to my own efforts but now it doesn't happen for if I spread my knowledge, I gain more workload. The one who makes the rest of us tired is the lead in the department. He, however, doesn't seem happy either. He must work long hours with no payment increase and he is a maintenance beam in name only. Should I endure this for the sake of a right to be on the door of leading in where no one truly has any investment? It doesn't seem prospering to me to do so. I could have the wealth of a retired person, but I am not permitted to spend my earnings in that way. The level of restraint is so restrictive I have to share my allotment with those in my home who have not earned the wage. Nor have they stayed in a personal relationship to me. It is all a loss, when I think on it. I never envisioned the labor I would have to endure, nor did I think I was the only one who saw this strain. I believed many were seeing as I did; yet, no one acted as though it was wrong or out of character. Where did the knowledge of operating for a better way end? Did that vanish into thin air as the people who no longer are here? Where is the attending Physician who made mankind in His image? Aren't we the same as before just different hosts of the physical body? Are not our hearts just as valued as the ones who were taken up? Did all things right and true disappear that day? Should I stay in need for all time or is there a new outlook I could present? What would happen to me if I did? For there is no opportunity within reach where I can claim the beauty of a unity I look at as righteous. God made man to have abundant favor; so I was led to hear. What then is this time frame I live within? Is it a total bend in the true nature of the one called Christ? Should I attempt to find the way to Him on my own value system? Is there an open-door policy I haven't heard of? Should I take into account He already paid the price for me? Isn't that what the cross represents? Is the whole idea a strange endeavor that needs a plan of action for it to be understood? Should I look in my grandmother's mirror and find her courage as my own? Can it even take form within me? Does the lineage of a person guarantee the right to know God? Should this be my hope? What is the truth of these thoughts of mine? How do I know what is just and good? Did God abandon me due to no action of prayer? Would He be so harsh? What must I do to entertain Him in the physical body? Does the value of me have no meaning? Where will I find the unity claimed by Scripture? God is all-knowing. At least that is what I was taught so why am I never in the know too? Should I dare to think He is far above me in that I am only able to breathe life due to His stand on my person? Can there be justice in this? Should I attend a ritual of some kind? Would a sacrifice make it somehow worthy? What would I even do for such a thing? Animals are now scarce due to depopulation, so I have nothing but bugs to offer. Isn't this against the policy of the one leading mankind today? A living Bible isn't allowed so how do I invite God to me? Will He call me to Him or am I without knowledge for all eternity?

Where is my heart today if not in my own unity? Does it matter I have never believed in the One who made me? Is it even vital I say a prayer or is there never to be the unity I hope to gain? Why do I press forward when no hope is before me? I have no doubt there is something to learn in the Scriptures but where am I to find the truth? God has not offered to me the unity I thought He would when I took Him as a witness, but I didn't think I had to surrender my heart to Him. Does He have the faith bucket necessary to gain or am I just alone and don't realize I am in need of Him? Have others fought to gain the Scriptural way and not said anything for the fact they will be killed? Is it enough to accept the Word but not apply it? How do I find the way ahead when I don't know where to find the gift of light? Has there been any kind of unity before this? I bear witness to the level of knowing God is real but why should I be made to witness the growth of no aid? I haven't offered another the Gospel. Is this why no recognition comes to me? Did I not offer hope so therefore I now get none? Is this the unity spoken of from on high? Where should I profess my love if there is no open path to do so? Does God hear me even when I think and ponder? Would it be right to stand on the offered trust just the same? What is the level one must achieve in order to claim the vital gain offered from God? Did I not carry forward the truth due to no ability or simply because I wanted my own way in life? Did God have a better formula for me to follow? Should I now think as to where to find a work of Him that will carry me onward to the way of hope? Is the work of another good enough to gain by or is it foolishness? I have the courage but not the answer for I did not pay attention to the offered hope my grandmother shared. I trusted she knew what she spoke of but where did it apply to me? I never requested the answer to knowing how to gain salvation due to my own idea I was good enough. I wasn't one to steal or shoplift. I never murdered anyone, nor did I stand in the way of someone finding happiness on their own merit. I believed I could review my plan at any time, so what did it matter if I invested or didn't? Wouldn't God still love me just the same?

Robin (Rochel) Arne

2

Seeking the Love of the Savior

Today I heard a verse from memory. Why now did this happen? Was it a gift or did I simply remember with no intent? Did God grant me the option of hearing or was the manner just simply my own thought process? Does it matter whether I thought of it, or if Christ gave it to me? Where and what should happen now? Do I find a place to align myself with this new understanding or have I already verbalized the needed stand? Should I look to some other kind of guiding light or is this what it will represent? Am I the one who needs to take the next step or did I claim the verse from my heart? Will I know the needed plan? Is there one? I have always thought God would not forget how to prosper His many. Am I one of them? Should I simply abstain from further idea making or did this start a chain reaction? Am I qualified to obtain the next expression or am I too weak? Did God grant me favor or am I simply hoping He did? I think about the recognized unity and ponder where it is to lead. I thought it would be more of an invite than a simple acknowledgement of character. I believe I witnessed a miracle, but now how should I entertain it? Did I value it enough? Is there more to the invite than a simple acknowledgement God is saving my heart? Should I accept the invitation? Will it be that simple? I should have opened the way in prayer and then maybe that would have made a difference. Right now, I am unsure as to what I am to do. My grandmother would have understood what transpired and I would have had an answer. Knowing where to tread is not always the way we think. I believe enough to answer the recognized gesture, but will it make a difference? Have the professions of others been this simple? Is my heart truly vested in this idea? Is there something more I need to do? Did God love me through this notion? Is He that caring and holy that no amount of money is needed to invite Him forth into my being? I would hope for some kind of insight, but should I wait? What will happen if I do accept Him in this way? Is it something I will always remember, or will it in time fade? I have no one to offer this plan toward so it is me alone who must decide. Going to the core of the unity is where I hope to reside. In the event I am wrong won't it mean heaven is out of reach? Should I accept my death is on the horizon? Will this be the end of me? What is the plan I need to pursue? Going in the way of faith has brought mankind into war and loss, or so it would seem. Yet, I see where the need to act is within me. I haven't offered my idea to another, but I would like to share the acknowledgement. Time is not the same as it once was. Many have been slain due to not renouncing the love of Christ. It is a public display and I find it hard to envision I must suffer in this way. Man has determined God is not worth dying for, but what about the many that have? Did they see what I do not? Was there a message they sent in the death of a martyr? I don't know where to stand on this new idea. It is not what I expected to happen, something tangible for me to entertain. The words came in a quiet endearment. I wasn't afraid or lacking in the unity. It was special and unique with character and love. How it gave me understanding was within my person. I thought I would cherish it, but now I stand unsure. Should I have enough momentum to stand in the quiet and pray from the perspective I heard the One who made me? Does this mean I have unity to Him? Am I now in the crowd of the living? How would I decipher such a thing?

    I believe I am not one to think too long about a subject, but this concern is a unique gift to ponder. The love of the One who made mankind has interrupted my thought process and drawn me to Him. How did this happen? When I thought all was forsaken, He came and captured me. Am I sure of this? I don't have another explanation as to why it happened. Yet, I stand unsure, and wondering did it even really happen? I think mankind has a Savior who cares for him. I should investigate this idea but how and where to learn? I love the idea I can hear from God. He never divulged Himself to me that I remember but if I paid more attention then maybe I would know for sure. I think I have the notion to offer my heart to Him, but I am not all together sure I can do it. I like the idea of knowing the King of man but is He safe to learn from? Did He sacrifice Himself for me to be with Him at heaven's doorway or did He only make me a slave to Him? Should I look to accept Him in a free manor with no strings attached or do I need to offer some kind of retail gift? I haven't understood what changed but I said in my heart "Lord, take me I am yours." I didn't think it would matter but now I am realizing it may have. It was a gesture I heard my grandmother proclaim so I invested and took action. Was there really a change due to this acknowledgement? Did I gain the witness necessary to obtain the unity I was hoping to find? What now? Did it actually transpire, and did it make a difference for all time? I never believed I could simply invite God into my heart. It seemed so misguided due to the available knowledge I had. I never dreamt I would have to say something so simple to gain hope but now I have the notion to share light to others. Did I really change? Am I a caring person today due to this stand? Should I tell others about it? Could it mean I have the ability to guide in a way I hadn't thought of? So much to consider but I do feel as though I need to enlighten others. Will I sacrifice my own life for another? It is all so new and undetermined at this time. Thinking about how God showed me the verse I now believe it was Him who stood with my heart. The opportunity came when no one was at my place of residence, so I had time to bend a knee and accept God as my own. It was a decision I made due to the value of the care I witnessed on behalf of my grandmother. I knew she believed, and it was real to her to say the prayer before me. Had I truly stood in the quiet and accepted the love I would not be in this situation today. However, here I stand now waiting for the next thing. What will it look like? Will some dark idea come as well, or have I now been adorned with only light? I walk with care, and I lead with little unity, as I have only just accepted Jesus as my Savior.

Trust has been difficult for me in the past. I have had relationships that soured, and I was left hurt and afraid. Is this the same or is God unique in He never hurts man in the manner of no guiding or instruction. God leads with purpose I believe and how this is known I do not comprehend. Did the stand of acceptance make the meaning clear to me or did I gain this perspective when I believed? How do I invite God to fill me with character and hope? Do I simply say the words and he hears or is there some other form of communication? I have taken to prayer in a subtle manner due to it being against the law for me to do so. No other I know of is a witness to God but there must be some others somewhere. Are we connected somehow? Should I ask and let them come to me? Would this change our way of acting to one another? Little gestures come at times from my heart I don't recognize. It is new to have an idea of hope and yearning. I should have read Scripture to gain the way of God. It would have meant I wasn't acting on my own merit. I now accept God can do great, wondrous things so I am ever waiting for more knowledge. I look to God for my intake, as I no longer have my Bible. If He could deliver one verse to me, he is able to prosper me again. I have the knowing aptitude to call on Him, but should I speak freely or is that too informal? Is God supportive to the one who speaks his mind, or does He get offended and strike out? My grandmother said He was a loving creature of beauty and care, never harsh but He does reprimand. What would a God of love have for a person such as I? Would He love me even though I haven't knelt and prayed in a certain way? I think I will begin to bow before Him where able and thank Him for the message of light He granted. That should be a good start to our bond of insight.

Do I now possess the ability to commit a plan of insight? Am I a holy person? Did I learn the true nature of God in one simple asking? Is He that good to His people? Were the minutes of hard thought making what did the maneuver or did it happen due to faith? Where shall I look for another offered hope? Will it come like it did or will there be another offering in a different nature? Should I believe I am not without hope? Am I the one now to determine where to step for another? What does it mean to be a witness for God? Do I have to attempt to stand in the way of teaching or is this too much for today's knowledge? Man needs the hope I have been given, but how shall I make it clear to anyone other than a team of people looking for answers as I am? How shall I know them? Will God make it clear to me who they are and how to support them? Is the unity still a part of this process or have I no other gain to come? Where is the pattern of favor for I am in need of more hope? It is hard to stand on such a simple undertaking, but it has been a bright spot where no other resided. God is not one to fake something so generous. I didn't remember love being so hope filled. Should I document the sudden endowment or is there more support to come? I look at faith and believe I have been given the hope of life eternal. Am I just simply now someone who has believed and finding favor or is this the way of being fed? Is God my support beam or will this courage fade and I lose my witness? I think there is more to this than I understand at this time. Leading is not my way of being for I never held a position of merit. I felt as though others were more inclined to stand in the idea of insight. Politicians have always been wealthy and with options of meeting many due to their social standing. Would it matter if I shout to the people in a direct way? Is this the hope I need to operate in so others learn from my hand? Can I be discrete and perform it in another aptitude? Should I look at others and now invest in where I offer a gentle outpouring of favor and watch to see who else supports this behavior? God has led me with true love. This I know as I had none prior to the asking. I believe I have become one of His and I enjoy the idea I am more secure.

"Teach me, oh God of light," is my battle cry. I aim to know Him in a greater way thus gaining a better unity to Him. I work with more knowledge He is all He professes to be. Where is the number of the people who also believe and have gained in support due to the acceptance of Jesus? Should I stand in honor of those who came before me? Is that how it comes forward? I think I am to realize God is the redeemer not mankind. I am often in the company of many who feel little to no value as they are under the duress of long hours and little hope. No bounty is put in motion and man finds no support for his investments. I have faith in the way I pray but not so much I believe I am all-knowing. God is the one who maintains my spirit. How this came to be was a simple acknowledgement He is the way. I never dreamt I would have the connection I do. It builds with the love of God growing in such a way I believe more richly. How should I apply this knowledge? Where do I set my heart now that it is whole and complete? Even though I struggle with the nearness of loss I feel smitten with support. If I have to offer another the rich belief, I have within it will mean another has found unity. This I hope to offer for many in need. Currently all of man is under the host of deception due to the false Antichrist. I see him for what he truly represents, which is harm to all. I now understand what his accomplishments are. They are to destroy everyone in his path. God is the opposite of this. With Him there is hope and a build of character pointing to the light for mankind to gain. The enemy wants all of man to die and lose salvation. He is a committed being of dark enterprising. I will not give him any acknowledgement for he is small and insignificant. He has no control over me for I know the real God of all. He is perfect and true with prosperity for man. I am part of the ministry known as the saving way. I believe God is working within my heart to explore my understanding and guide it with clarity. I never felt as comforted as I do today. The nature of my unity is God alone within me. This is priceless and true. No other can mend my spirit in the same manner as a justified God of hope. I believe I have witnessed the guiding favor of true love. I shall forever feast on the One who made me from dust.

 I am here not feeling so lost or forsaken. In the balance I now have a partner who embellishes me with favor. It is a spiritual presence within not that of feelings or notions not understood. The quiet is not harming me for I stand with a guide leading me to a better thought process. I have not been without courage since finding God. In the unity I have a path of hope. I never know when I will be found out, but I have hidden myself with character. I reached out to another who seemed to bear fruit, but I have not taken it further than a smile and nod. Does it look to be the end of humanity? I do not know the plan of the Most High but I have faith He is working to guide me just the same. The limit of God is not a real thing. He is able to protect me from any outstretch of harm. But I know I may be left on the battlefield of dark intent. It is the way of life today. Had I but accepted the love of God before this era I would be standing in a better way. God did not stop me from knowing Him intimately. It was my reserve that caused me to fail. I used to think harm would come my way if I surrendered to God my faith but today, I see it is the path to life eternal. The character of God is right and true. There is none better. How does this mean something without guiding light? It doesn't for God the Father has shown me a better way. How do I share this knowledge? Should I write it on the bathroom wall? Would that make it more visible, or would there be a camera watching my every move? I do not know what the Lord would desire of me to bear witness to Him by, but I trust a door will present and I will enter through the passageway. To follow God for the love of Him is a build in where we are tied in hope not that of gain in the pocketbook. It is something new to me to feel so valued. God is pure hope in this, I am sure. He has given me the insight of His character and I lean into this with support. The Holy One of pure knowledge is all I am in need of. Why is there no offering of Him from the people remaining since the uptake of loss in numbers? I do not pretend to understand all the will of God, but I do know He values me above all else. Every person on earth can have the same gift. I know this to be true. How does the market not fail with so little comfort? I believe man has the garnering of value. He just needs to apply it to the One who made him. To place your heart in the hands of the One who places value to your person is a sight none can compare with. This I have learned due to God, Himself, serving me in favor. How can such a simple investment bring such a great return? Only God with His miraculous way of being could be so generous. I have the will to follow Him and to learn more about His person. If He guides me, I will follow. I have the will to walk with character due to his presence within me. Such a unity I cannot express but I know it is real. The pathway has come into play, and I am thankful. Shelter now resides within my heart not the structure of a building. God is perfect and good. He maintains my heart and He works with my outlook. I know I am weak, but I gain in prayer and trust by placing my desire toward the love of Him.

I am grafted to the Father who has prepared for me to know Him in a personal way. How this came to be is not for me to discern. I am capable of unity today due to the understanding I am not alone any longer. I thank my God for His care and support. In Him I have faith and trust built in the way of prayer and standing in favor of His counsel. Jesus is the one who maintains my heart. I have the gift of hope residing in my spirit and now I know there is a better way. God provided me with support even though I cherished Him not. He stood in the way of the enemy and took me to Him. I did not call to Him in hopes of a reward. It was pure hope that came forth. I desired a better way of life not knowing where it would take me. Now I realize the passion of God is what carried me to Him. He has a gift of unity none can compare with. In knowing Him I have favor abundant. It is by His witness to my spirit I thrive for there is only death and destruction in my setting. People today are not in the manner of leading for the care of others. The whole attempt to lean into another has been washed away by deceptive values placed upon each person without the unity to Christ. Even if this time frame had not come into play it would stand true for those in need of salvation. God provided me with support where I now know He is the great way of being. He is holy and good, and I never desire a different substitute. God is the character of a tried Being of knowledge. He holds mankind in the palm of His hand. I am not standing in the light due to my own effort. It is God, Himself, who has the plan. In the mention of His name, I could be put in chains; yet, I would have Him for my support beam. He never fails a person in need. I may have to suffer but none can claim me against my Father. Knowing the way to stand has been a birth I was in need of having. God is the one who made me complete. I now long for the way of Him for all time. There is none who shield me but my Caregiver, the Risen Savior. Jesus is the one who died for me at Calvary. This has been something I appreciate and now have knowledge of due to the grace of God's inherit ability to speak to my heart. His Word is alive, and it stands even though no one has the support of the written Counsel.

Today I heard a verse I remembered from long ago. How this comes to be I do not know but I love I hear it so clearly. God, the one who made me, is never in lack of knowledge as to how I am feeling and what I am thinking. His goal is always the same, I know Him in an abundant way. He is perfect and a calm reflection. I gain when I operate as He does. I do not know all the details and how it all comes into play, but I believe this era is the end of days. Revelation comes to me in pieces. I hear a message and know it is right when my heart is embraced and at peace. If there is doubt, I do not put much stock in it. To love God above all is something I have to offer, and I stand in hope and harmony. God is the one who developed me, so I am not one to offer another idea. People in need see themselves without hope but when God is the focal point true hope resides. I cannot fathom how I functioned before I knew the love of the All Mighty. I have the faith needed to move a mountain due to His character not my own. To love Him and place hope toward His heart is gain for me not just recognition to Him but for an all-encompassing value. I should have understood there was so much more to knowing the One of light than just a committed presence. If I had the option to claim God as a newborn I would but there is no turning back time. The light of the One who made all things right and true is everywhere if one has Him within. I now see people in a new way. They have meaning to me rather than just being of the same species. It took time for me to grasp I may never have a companion who shares this knowledge but in truth I am not in need of another's company. God has provided me with the love of Him and it upholds my spirit.

God is the one who made heaven and earth, in doing so we now have a delight in the heavens above. The earth is not tarnished but it is without the love of many. People are finding no value to their way of being due to false authorities lording their stand over them. But I have found the truth and in doing so I am able to withstand the lie and temptation, to avert my heart from the false leader and grow in the name of Jesus. I thought knowing God would be hard and with no knowledge. I stood against myself in this thought process. The truth of Christ is that man is better to know Him. The value of the saving power is not something given out of duty but rather that of a holy, sound manner. God supports the love of many. He is not simple or in need of any insight for He is complete knowledge and character in the righteous form of hope. Leading is a way of the past but I lean into God for this acquirement. God is perfect and in the knowing of His person; I find unity completes His makeup. He never has attempted to restrain my behavior, but I now desire to walk in an upright way. I enjoy doing good and walking by faith. It means I have the trust to God I dream of. The level of commitment is building. I value my Savior more each hour and minute for He captures me in my heart never forsaking me or causing harm. What better way than to commit to the One who made mankind in His image?

The One to determine where to walk is the great Waymaker of light. I have the knowledge God is who he claims to be. Not from my own heart but placed there when I believed in Him. How does this happen I am not sure of? I value the Savior above all things, and I stand in the way of faith to Him. Knowing Him as the One who made me is a sight of birth I favor. God above is all-knowing, and He leads with character. In Him is the unity I needed and now have. Thanking Him is all I have to offer. My wealth is stolen and not my own. If I withdraw a sum, it is questioned, and I must prove what the sum was for. I have no hope of having a fortune, as it all goes to the governing body of people. I know nothing of others than they are not a true counsel of support. I have the aptitude to teach another; but where will it get me? A tighter unit of labor, which I know I won't build from, so there is no benefit. However, if I can manage to align myself with someone looking for the saving power of truth, that would engage my heart and lead me to a better forward intent. To love the way I offer fruit is not my own manner. But the lead of God for many I hope to achieve. In the market is the way of sight due to a lead of no value; yet, in the way of study I have little to share. I record the verses as they come, and I am grateful I gain them in faith. How am I to offer this course of learning? Should I hang a shingle on my home, or would it simply mean death in a quick way? I like to love others now and I have a plan to speak to some of my coworkers, the ones who seem to have some kind of heart within them. I don't know where I will get the courage but I trust God to offer me this ability. He has honored me in knowing about Him, so I believe He will pave the way for me to unite with another for the sake of His name. I have the opportunity to light a path for another; yet, how do I attempt this act? The process of leading always seemed so difficult to me but now I feel more enabled. The value of support from on high is not a simple gesture that is fleeting, but rather that of a knowing ability for my heart. I value the way God moved in my spirit and I plan to offer it to others who are willing to acknowledge me in the slightest way. I am thinking they are not altogether without hope. The many before me are not often carrying the intent of a good neighbor but rather that of a different affront. They have the desire to gain for self and not that of another but where is the offered gain then? I have valued my own understanding and found it faulty, not fruit bearing. I plan on divulging this and seeing where it takes my voice. The guide of the Holy One is what I yearn to imply. Will He stand with me on this? I believe He will not only aid me but grant me hope in the commitment. The truth of what I offer is for all who would claim the light for themselves. Should I set up a stand of some kind in the break room or would this mean I die suddenly? The gamble is high. Should I implore to another my insight and wait for God to offer him my understanding? If no hope unfolds does this mean I am without the saving witness, I dream of? I do not understand where to walk but I know God is in my favor. This is something I envision in a sound manner. How did this happen with such an inspiring gift? Only God knows the answer to this question. He has made within my heart the hope of many to find Him in a favoring response. His call is heard where the mind accepts it as good. Little growth has been in my history. I never invited the work of God to me but now I savor it. God has led me with support, and I now have the idea of Him garnering me to salvation. I did not fail to invite Him into my person; I just didn't claim this growth until He brought me to Him. The invite was clear, and I knew to reject it meant total death and this I did not want to happen. I have the ignition switch of a grant of strength, and I can offer another the same unity. It isn't weak within but there are many variables as to what may happen. I need to realize I may no longer have freedom of any kind. Though now the only light is from God. There remains the solution within my heart, but I am not one to jump quickly or without prayer. To value life is knowledge but to offer it to serve God is new to me. I love the Father and I cherish this unity so what will it mean if I no longer can be alive? Is life eternal all there is and what does it look like? My grandmother was able to discern when to speak and how to invite others to know God but today we are to be silent with no guiding. Does this qualify as outreach even though I haven't spoken to anyone? Do my prayers stand as a witness to God? Is He faithful to the one who shares a ministry with no action in the way of voicing His name? Where do I operate as a team member to Him? Are we tied still in the way of faith? I am unsure how to profess this to Him; yet, I know He hears my heart, so I am not hiding anything from Him. He supports me with the unity, and I believe He will not fail to guide my idea making.

My faith is not my own for God delivered it to me. How did this even come into view? Where is the origination but not that of Christ Himself? I have always assumed God would know how to operate wherever I was stepping but now I have learned God carries me over the difficult terrain. I am not one to attempt to stand where there is a line of fire but today it appears there is no other way. I have no ability to outlay the perfect support, so I stand on the few notes I have taken when a vision of support from on high has happened. I did see a cast of unity in the way it was shown so I knew I wasn't daydreaming. I was awake and my faculties were sound. I have never had such a notion to share as I do now. However, it is difficult due to the stand of the governing body of fake authorities. They have no idea I am supporting others at this time. I work like usual, but I am now fed in the heart with a sight of inspiration. I have the level of consciousness supporting others where I lean into God for unity. I love Him and I serve when the door is open to do so. No one seems to accept my little outreach and so far only the quiet have looked toward me for gain. I have no conversations to express for fear of being found as a believer. This is not acceptable by the people in charge. If you have faith outside the government, you are considered a problem citizen, so you are taken to the gallows and executed. People stand upright and claim Jesus to the one's witnessing the execution. I have the knowledge they are openly viewing possibilities, but I have never seen one happen. I do not like dark scenes and images, so I had no inclination to go to such an event. But there are many who have shared the outcome of the fallen as that of Scripture being given and spoken. Why does God not step forth and stop this calamity? Is there a purpose to the days we are living? Has mankind been so harsh it is needed for a cleansing of the care to be bright once more? I should remember the verse of redemption but as of now I haven't understood it. The term is new and only just received but I invest in trust and wait for God to speak. Will He continue to share our hearts or is this the only unity I will inherit? It is gold to me so I believe God will offer more in the way of trust. He is good and I know He desires for me to witness the love of many. How can I offer true knowledge if I, myself, do not know the way ahead? Is there a certain way to accept this truth? Have the written documents been stored in a vault or am I to get glimpses at a time for gaining hope? The will of Christ is for His children to love and have unity to Him, but with today's way how can this happen? If death comes before I admit Him to another, will I still enter heaven's pathway? Should I not lead at least one person to God to be saved? Is this a condition I must meet? Do I need to know the answer to gain entry in the skyway of life? I am not one to ponder for fear of losing the love I already found so I look to what I have learned. God is good and righteous bearing so to know another in faith would be a blessed unity. This I can surmise with love and honor.

God is ever supportive of my fear. He leads me to a calm presence even though I have no authoring of His stand in I simply believe and find Him a gift to my heart. He is always there whenever I need to think of something prospering to me. He lets me hear His voice in subtle underlining ways. I have the notion He can offer many the same thing. I stand in support of the faith I have gained; yet, I desire to share this knowledge to all who come my way. I don't require a microphone but if given the opportunity I would shout it to the world. The way of knowing you are given hope is for there to be a day of bright thought processes without even having to ask for such a thing. God is the way to prosperity. This I learned the day I offered myself to Christ. It was such a simple thing; yet, so powerful. The love and care I now embrace was something I had lost faith in but now I am complete in my desires. I have little accounting practices so I can't relate it to dollars and cents, but I know it far exceeds the love of money. The way of evaluating the goal of righteous living is not for the one who only dreams of wealth. To know you must exist with cash flow means you realize the truth of a committed work ethic. But I have found the truth of love, and it far surpasses that of leading for the sake of no intent. To work for the value of offering another the love you have found is to prepare the heart for a better way. Leading is something I never thought I would do but today I hope to offer all I can a gift of support. The unity of Christ is fair and true and there is nothing more valuable than Him. I offer man no value on my own merit but to share the love of God is fruit to the heart. This is the truth of care at its finest.

God is magnificent and true. This has come to me by way of inspiration not my own undertaking. How do I ever put forth the knowledge I have? Is there to be something coming I am not aware of? Should I offer a program in the way of a commitment that supports the love I have to give? Would a hug be a gesture I could offer? Would such a thing be accepted today in the time of black leading? Where is the plan I am to follow? I have no guide just the spiritual way but that is quite enough as I am fed with light in the manner of it. Look at the many that have fallen and see where it has taken them. No hope is present, and I alone hear the voice of reason. But maybe there are others pretending not to know who God is to them. Could it be I simply need to stand in the presence of my coworkers and align to them what I have learned? Should I announce it to the office in a meeting? Would this stand as the way ahead? I do not intend to lose my insight, but I look forward to the day I can announce to all who my Savior is to me. The love He has shown is far reaching and within my heart I hear His way. I am led due to the wise stand I made on His behalf. Does He require my action in support or is it enough I now know Him and call Him Savior? I invite the thought of another coming to Jesus so I can correlate to him how I interpret the love of God to me. I never believed I was without hope but now I recognize I was. The former me is now forgotten; yet, still I am the same person. How can this even compute? God has such a nature that holds man in a bounty and a manner of true love giving all the opportunity to gain Him within. Such a loving God I know!

God the one who made me is all I think of these days. It was such a simple gesture to Him; yet, I am in complete honor of His presence within me. It would not be so important but now I understand I would have perished and gone to hell had I not accepted God's saving power. The streambed is holy from Him to me, and I shall honor the flow with character. The simplest of gestures brought me to Him and I shall always be thankful. God is not one to align Himself if you are not willing to know Him. I learned this from the prior way I acted toward Him. I was not interested in serving Him and I stood at a distance in darkness so as not to know Him personally. What a mistake I made in that thought process! But today, due to accepting Jesus as Lord, I have purpose and hope within not just thoughts of gain in a material way but rather for the refreshing bounty of favor from on high. God's gift of His Son was such a price that none can compete with it. What a suture to mankind! I have the insight of hope due to God placing it within me and I engage with Him all the more. I believe the power of Christ is a sight plan that teaches me where and how to operate. Little advancements happen and I reflect on how God orchestrates my will. I have freedom to reject the presence but what good would it be? I know to trust God is the better path for me.

Glory is not something I can relate to. I was never the popular person on the block but now I realize to share light to another brings the One who crafted me honor and this is meaningful. The love of me to God is all I care about and to share this knowledge I aim to do. God is supportive of all mankind, so I want to explain this to many. How will I be able to do it? I shall wait with expectation for I know God is the King and He can do all things good and right. To share the love of Him is His goal for my life and the fact I am willing to stand on His behalf speaks to the grace and care of Him through me. Little glimpses have come to me as to how to invest in the care of another. I can place a slim gesture of spoken words or perhaps ask someone to call forward their offered insight so I can share mine as well. What would this mean for my days ahead? Would I be tried and hung from the rafters above? Would it be a witness, or would I fail and lose my heart in the action of death? I believe God will gift me the ability to stand for Him whether I am alone or in the midst of many for He supports the voice of unity with clarity. I have the unity I longed for, and I now invite God to show me how to operate so I can lead others to Him. Will I favor them when it happens or will I cave and lose my strength? With the Word of God comes a presence of knowledge I didn't know was possible to contain. Titles mean something; yet; I am the one who gained in the view of my knowing the Savior. I became a member of the saving way. Is there a term for this? Should I ask Christ who I am to Him? Do I have meaning in His heart as I believe I do? Light is here; and yes, I am cherished by Him! What a wonderful truth. I shall tell another what I learn and wait to see what comes from it. I will either gain a friend or lose my life, but what matters is I speak the care I have gained to another. Life here, in this time frame, is dark and I look for another to gain in faith. God will enable me to speak. I believe this with my whole being! He is faithful. This I have learned.

God is a spokesman to me. In His favor I have complete trust and guiding from His hand. I am not without fear but no one other than Him is my gain. I know I have the right to walk away at any point but what would it gain me? I have the idea I would become as the lost are and drift with no hope once more. To offer the love of Christ to my heart means I can stand in the wake of a wave. The value of the One who made heaven and earth is far superior to that of a simple standing in questioning. I have the power of the Almighty and I know I can offer it to others. I mean to do this where I am given the opportunity. The stand I now support is for my own value to be gifted light but in doing this act I stand for Christ. I have never before accepted such a unity and there never will be another as rich. I believe the value of knowing the One of character is far superior to that of a life without His love and hope. To align my heart with Him is truly the better way I have found to breathe life worth living. God has the unity I need to be complete, so I know I am in good hands. Accepting Him was the best gift I could ever have invited to me. I alone have no support but with God there is a great witness to my heart and I am able to offer this guiding way to another. The unity I have is ever before my way and I tie to it with trust.

Glory is for the One who made me not the people who act as though I don't have a meaning of light. The value of me is far above that of what man thinks or deems prospering for only God is the way to life eternal. I look at where man has been driven in his own value system, and I see the loss he put forth. The unity to him is not whole and it won't ever be without the caretaker of Christ within him. I now am a being of insight and I stand in the manner of true hope. How this came to be was a dream from on high.

God loved me and stood for my own way to acquire Him as the One I invest in. I love Him with all I have to offer and in doing this action true support is garnered. Where will I have the way to present to others this knowledge, I do not know but I have God as my hope so I know it can be offered? Days of work have meant I claim my King as my Savior and in doing this act I remember I am fed by Him. He is masterful and good. He leads me with hope and light and this means so much more than the gift of a wage. All I have within me is tied to His person. Gone is the rush of funding my account. What stands in its place...the plan of knowing many find the prosperity I have been given. It is a knowledge that needs broadcasting but how do I go about this? God will lead and there will be a day where I offer hope to one in need. God knows how to align me with another who will offer some kind of incentive for me to reach out to him with care. It can be something minor and in the making of a friendship. I know I don't have to offer wealth to gain the hand of mercy. He does not require for me to lend money to others for the sake of building Him in awe. That is not how He operates. Many used to impress to people that giving cash was the way to inherit the kingdom of God. But in truth it was a deceptive measure to gain the payment of wealth in a lying way. God is true to His character and in offering free knowledge is the way to align the heart to others with unity. God supports any effort made to give another the intent of Him for the care of it and not the reward.

Today was unusual, as I had the notion something was amiss. A partner at the workstation I entail came to me with a question about where I get my joy. It was not something I expected but the guide within told me to stay clear of this question. I did not offer a hope to him but stood with the knowledge he has seen the light within me. This came as a surprise, but I was not withheld on my own understanding; so I know protection was incorporated. I now know God will share me where it will be a guiding hope and not a loss. How do I justify not speaking when the question was posed? The Holy One of insight guided my thought process and I clearly realized something fowl was underway. I am secure knowing God will care for me in such a manner. It is a calm unity I hadn't expected to realize. God has the perfect way of speaking, so I gain from Him. I thank Him for this daily. The One who made my heart has it soundly taken care of within His way of goal making. I now can rest in an assured way. I have the goal of knowing where to offer my light. It came to me while I was dressing for the day. I will say a quiet welcome to the one who offered a smile and in doing this act I will let the light glow. Knowing I can simply say a gift of insight guides me with respect to God. He doesn't declare I must offer my head on a platter rather He provides an opportunity so I can be safe; yet, administering hope. God cares about every facet of my spirit. He knows I am not of the nature to physically engage in a fight to the death, so He has offered me a quiet gain to witness with. I praise Him all the more for this favor!

The love of God flows forward in where all I own; I offer His way. Should I add my very heart to Him with a notation I am all in? This is what it means to truly love the great One of all! Standing so another can hear the sound of God to him is a gift I relish in. I just gifted a question to another about salvation and he didn't back away. He accepted the question with a will I haven't seen prior in him. Did God open the pathway, or did I just hit him at the right time in his thinking? I believe God was the one orchestrating the lead and I feel secure that what I said went into the spirit of the one I witnessed to. He was a man of support for my desk area. He didn't come forth but looked at me with character, so I know something registered. Was it a test of strength, I portrayed, or did I fail in saying so little? He did not complain or report me to the authorities for posing the question to him. But when I went to find him later, he was preoccupied with another so there was no opportunity to engage once more. I trust the Lord in His offered hope and I pray the individual finds unity in the quest. I have the notion a stirring will happen, and he will either accept God, becoming a follower or I will find my desk vacated and my forward path will end at the company. Either way I have stood on behalf of God for another which is what I plan on doing where able. Should this be my final acknowledgement to the page of writing it means I have fallen prey to the authority of the Antichrist, and I am no more alive. But it will then be I have found the favor of God, and I am in heaven with Him for all time. The value is far greater than the commission so I will press forward and continue to stand for my Savior, Jesus.

True meaning is found in the care of God, and this is for certain within me. Today I found the faith landed with unity. The man I witnessed to in secret has given me a calling card, a simple gesture of favor by smiling in my direct line of viewing. I believe he has accepted the fact I am here to aid him in his journey of faith. How will this be, I do not know but I do realize I have accomplished something on behalf of the saving witness I was given. The realization God has carried me farther and He has invested in my outreach means I am truly supporting Him for many. Even though it was one individual meeting of the heart I now understand others can have the same knowledge. The unity now stands between us, and I hope to offer him more encouragement. I do not know if he has accepted the One who blends the heart to Him, but I believe he is pondering it just the same. I will work with hope and look at how I can obtain another opportunity to witness something meaningful to him. God has the structured way of being light and He will offer to me a way ahead in this idea I hold. To know the One who made man is to believe He is good at all times. I have an abundant thought process and in the manner of favor God has been calling me gifted. I know I am small at this time, and I need guiding, but I believe what I have learned can be shared freely. I look at how I am supported, and I desire for all to have the same insight. It is a birth of light that feeds the heart and conquers the darkness. Knowing the value of the One who made you is so rewarding none can compare. Does this mean I will fall short and lose my stand due to little instruction? I do not believe this is the case for I have never been as involved with others as I am today. Even though I must work in the quiet I pray constantly within.

God delivers to the one who believes and has the desire to obtain His way of being. In the manner of Him is support and faith. The glory of God is for man to have Him as his counterpart. To love the heart of man is not something all of man unites to. I now have the faith to offer others the unity of Christ due to Him being my all in all. I have forgotten where I fed my heart from days of old, but I know I wasn't willing to offer another time and invested care. I had my own unity, and I didn't look at the offering as of value. God, the one who made me realize there is a better way, took me in and gave me honor without pride or a diet of loss. With the support I bring, another has begun to stand as well. It happened right in front of me, and I added a message to the conversation. We spoke quietly and in the midst of the conversation another said a bright hope to our hearts. I do not know if this person has heard the wise God of all, but I believe God is moving in his path. Acknowledgement comes in the quiet and we work with character but not in the limelight. We know it would mean no offered goodness would be accepted. So, the way we connect is simple manners of hope. Such as a quick glance and nod to each other where no other views our intent. The longing I have to rush and hug this man is strong but that would mean jail for sure. I know he has the same inclination, and he stays at a distance, so we aren't found as law breaking. I believe once we get to have the ability to gain in the way of knowing how we have come to find the faith we will have the knowledge each has gained. And it will make us sturdy and more connected. But for now, I stand in the invite and wait for God's timing to happen before me.

For the man I found seeking me with the question of my joy he now has an attending manner toward my person. He asks on occasion if I would like to host him for a date or night of passion, but I stand away from this objective. I do not look at him with hope but rather of a loss in where he has no knowledge of God within him. I know it is a trap to investigate whether I conform to the role of sexual leading with no boundary, but I won't compromise this activity against my Lord. It is something of a new way of being. However, I never engaged in the manner of sex for the sake of the physical undertaking. It had to have meaning for me. A casual relationship was not my style but in truth it made no difference. It was still sin and I was just as stained as the man who looks at it as a conquest. To know the truth of support concerning marriage is a value I now hold. I don't have the idea of it happening as the law is against it, but I know to go against God in this way is not wise. I value the Father's love above the physical touch, so it may be God is working out the way for my heart to stand as a simple light with no tended love affair.

God is the way to thrive and have favor. It is not man's ability to make light happen. It is from God alone. In the manner of favor God supports any insight of light and hope. He is the one who made all things right and true. How can this be? He is unique and holy where man is not so to stand in His witness is sound growth. I love the plan of God for man to be tied to Him for all time. It is a trust born in the way of true hope and standing. I have the hope I am eternal due to the realization God can work a miracle for me where I cannot. The faith I build on in a daily basis is due to prayer and the way I receive Scripture from God. He is faithful to recite the hope to me even though I had forgotten what I was taught in my youth. I attended church for the action of meeting others but in the growing pathway my mind learned the true nature of the Risen King. I am grateful God perfected this for me as I no longer have a Bible to read. They have all been burned and any material relating to God is not law abiding to own. I believe many are hiding this gift but how do I find them? Are there any in my workplace? How shall I investigate them without leading the authorities to their doorstep? I would be crushed to hear of another faith bearer burned for their acknowledgement to God. It happens regularly but no one admits it. To go against the one claiming to be lord leads to a loss of life. He will accept no other in his place. I know he is unrighteous, and he acts as Satan, himself. To honor such a being is not what I am about but I know I will have to hide or take the lash if I refuse him. Going forward is not a stand that will be easy. I have the heart, but will fear overtake me? If God is the one leading, I will stand with courage and be able to gain even in death. I will not accept the mark as I know it means I have committed my heart to the evil being of falsehood. It is better to offer my life to God than to be under the arm of the Antichrist. He will never be able to cause me to regret the love I have for Jesus, but I do have concerns I will be judged and hanged because I support the Lord.

My fear is not as strong as it once was. I have the knowledge God is caring for me all the while. I believe I can thrive in this wait of no sight due to the ability of God to reach me with character traits leading to insight. I support the love of God and I place this before others. I do it in such a way that only the ones who themselves are not all dark find it a rewarding experience. We do not invest in friendships other than a smile in the direction of the eye. It means a chance to see clearly who believes and who is trying to gain. I know at any point I will be found as an aid that does not adhere to the plan of the enemy but until then I will try to defend my faith. Seeing others gain in the way of accepting the outreach has been a gift I needed to have. The love of the One who made us is at work, so we enter a comrade unity. I have been trying to find a way to express the unity I know is real but right now it is not clear as to how to do this maneuver. The One who stepped forward into the path was the first I found in response to trust. Jesus is this person. I developed a better understanding with the way I presented my heart and in the way of knowing the righteous offered aid came by my unity to Him. I love the goal of reaching another. It makes the day bearable. Where I am given the green light to further stand, I aim to enhance my trust and direct my work in that holy sight-plan. Knowing I have only a small unity does not scare me into silence. It rather draws me to the conclusion I have the author in my witness. God is the crafter of my learning. He gifts me more unity and I hear Him speak as to the way I should work. I have the knowing ability to abide in His manner and I believe I am grace to others. God is perfect and right. In Him is the knowledge of leading me so I don't lose my footing. Hope has an emblem of faith and in it I have the grasp of a witness with support. God the Father is always leading me in a quiet gain, and I thank Him for this gift.

I love the fact I have the manner of faith necessary to offer another the gift of support, but it is slim with little outreach. This is due to the level of security we must adhere to. I didn't offer my name, but I did place a gift of support in the mirror in the bathroom to a woman who needed a care in her direction. She saw the smile and returned it with caution. I may not have gifted her words, but she realized another held her in esteem. I know this is not a large outreach but today it is just as valued. To have no plan to share the Scripture I gain I can only share emotion in such a manner. God knows how to reach those I place my heart toward, so I trust His care and offer what I am able to give. If there is a possibility of sharing the gift of knowledge of truth I will step forth and place it forward. The knowing way of God indicates to me He will grant this growth and support will shine. I have the slightest of offers but the commitment I have is never ending. I watch and learn, and I see more than I used to. Another has stepped in my direct path, so I plan to see if there is a response to my signature witness. If he offers a glance and a nod, I will know there is hope within him.

I have dreamt of sharing the verse of Scripture pertaining to the love God has for mankind in where Jesus is declared the One of hope in the saving manner of blood shed for sin nature to be restored. It is a significant verse and the meat of the Gospel. I can recite it here though but for now not in public

16 "For God so loved the world that he gave his one and only Son, that whoever believes in him shall not perish but have eternal life. 17 For God did not send his Son into the world to condemn the world, but to save the world through him. John 3:16-17 NIV

Robin (Rochel) Arne

form
3

Belief Comes but Still the Pain is Here

    God is the one I care for more than mankind, but I know the heart of Christ is with His people and His desire is for them to find their way to His person. God is character and true love so I never have to wonder who I should pursue in the light of His amazing way. I walk with support, and I have the gift of insight in I am not standing in the dark concerning favor. He works through my heart and aligns the manner of Him to me. How does this work? I am not the one who determines it. God alone is the great I Am. No other is capable of doing such a feat. To value the One who made me is something I never used to ponder but now it is present on my mind. I accept I was not yearning for the great way of Jesus and due to my own value to me I missed the gateway to escape this terrible time on earth. In heaven I would be secure with the growing vision of pure gain. But now I am here trying to survive with little aid. God above is my mainstay and I thank Him for His honor to me. Taking into account He works on my behalf has provided me with unity to Him in a personal way. I love His character and I have the support I need to rest with comfort at bedtime. In my daily outreach, I am finding there are several willing to engage with actions not easily seen. We walk together in single file, but our hands stretch into the guard just enough we know we are intertwined. The care this gives is amazing even though it is such a simple gesture it makes us stronger. God is leading and showing us where to operate and how to plan for more standing. Today I was given the option of moving to another office ward, but I stood and said no. I desire to learn more for the sake of another in that when we connect, we find the unity God puts forth. I have the realization who has committed their heart to the One of hope and who is contemplating it. God speaks to me, and I acknowledge the weak with care. This aids the way they think and idea making happens. I connect with them once salvation comes to them and we offer each other the gift of outward love. It is simple gestures, nothing grand or in view of the managing body. We have the understanding our connection is not known to management. Such a gift is not forgotten, and we speak in the spirit one to another. This is a way to visualize the One who gave us hope. Our love stands in awe of God not in how we find ourselves. To gain from on high has been such a unity none other has given. We offer our heart in the direct path of God and in return He flourishes our idea making. I build in the heart today and I look to those who do as well. We plan in person how we can offer others this unity, but we must do it out of earshot of the developed guards and their stand in the building. Cameras are not in the rest area of the back door. It is a small landing, and we favor this location over the office park knowing that has many who hate mankind. It is proven due to the many that ventured out and found their lives taken. Why would a trip to open airway cause such alarm? No good thing is offered from mankind today. Only the one who believes understands this truth. The knit community is elect, and we are to support their every whim. It goes against my heart, but I have no choice but to conform. I pay my expenditures and I give where it is expected knowing it means nothing in the afterlife.

Trust has been placed to many who have the acceptance of God to their hearts. I know this happens and matters to the One who created our gift of salvation. Knowing the reward is so entrenched we needn't worry about forgetting where it came to be and how it happened. God has shown us who is faith bearing and who is not. This alone is proof God is all things right and good. To protect me in such a manner is a blessing I can't lose. I have now the option of forwarding this gain by standing in prayer to those I meet. The spiritual guiding is heard, and we join together to place the power of God before the heart. God has prospered us in the way of unity, and we aspire for those in the dark to come to the light. Only the one who shares a hope in some form do we intertwine with. Simple outward actions lead us to the idea of who is close to claiming Jesus and who is simply pretending. We do not offer a unity where no love is projected. God has guarded our hearts and shown us where to offer the lead. It is vital we stay close in this operating measure. Due to the plan of committing many to God we have not lost those who claim a hope in care. We see it before the outreach happens. It is a spiritual blessing, and we witness the birth with joy. Our hearts are joined when the individual accepts the saving One of good. It is not declared to us in a mouthpiece. It is a knowing that happens. We can understand their decision once it has happened, and we gain in the way of another for God. We thank the Lord and praise His holy way. I would not believe it, but I have now learned God works through the spiritual and not the physical alone. I have the gift of prophecy, so I know God shows me who is ready and where they are dining for light. I have the knowing ability to entertain the heart and offer it a secure thought implant. I pray with support, and I learn in the way of faith. It comes to me in spite of the officers and their peering eyes. I can see the one who is about to claim Christ for himself. In this knowledge, I unite and offer my understanding to him by way of support. Simple gestures are the key. Some are not as willing, and they lose the unity before salvation takes hold. When this happens, I wait for God and let Him act in the mind of the one seeking. I do not attempt to make anyone find the unity. It would only do harm. I know I am not the one who does the work but the Father and the Lord. It is in them the light happens within. I accept I am merely a partner in prayer and unity, not the one of hope. God has this role, not me.

    God offers me the way to know Him better as I move forward in faith. It is Scripture I enjoy getting as I know it is His personal gift to my heart. The witness I provide due to it is solid and in good standing. I allow myself the realization I am not all-knowing, and I have a lot to gain by being willing to learn from the heart. I have the knowledge He is ever within me and that aligns with the way I offer another His light. To love Him is a free gift and I desire to express the way for many. God is the way to survive this era of darkness. Without Him I would now be under the influence of the deceptive Antichrist. He has many who follow him due to the way he operates in hate. It is a surprise to me how many find the dark way of life to be a reward, but the true knowledge lies with Christ. Death is the way of the false god of man. He offers only loss and no real fruit of inspiration. I understand there are those still not committed either way but to not support Jesus is to stand against Him. Many do not realize this is the truth, so they think they are standing in the right path of a settled heart. Where there is deception, anger is present. Today a man with no hope infiltrated our harmony and we stood against him in prayer. We knew right from the start he was a liar and had ill intent in store. God gifted us the knowing way and we did not feed the well of deception. We acted as though we had no opinion when in reality; we desired to share the truth to those who were watching the event take form. However, it was not the reaction he was hoping to see so no harm came to us. We evade the people who have no hope, and we commit the felony of sight simply by standing on behalf of the One who created us. But we know the path with Him is bright and there is a sight we will be witnessed to that is just. God will work through us for the hour has not come for us to die. Until this happens, we are capturing the ones we find looking for hope. They aspire in the way of an outreach that is barely visible, but we witness it and know God gifted us the ability to see it. We thank Him for the opportunity to reveal to them who Jesus is. Scripture has come in the form of a thought I gained. I share it here.

10 Love and faithfulness meet together; righteousness and peace kiss each other. Psalm 85:10 NIV

The time to witness is always in the way of a unity that unfolds in some form. We have learned God is care to those who support Him in faith. When a dark thought enters our minds, we negate the idea and leave it in the wind. It takes discernment and we are gaining in the way of unity to it. We determine who is truly looking for faith and who pretends. We work as a team and investigate the lead as one. No one has more value than the other. We are tied with gold of true light and in the making of this unity we support each other. We do not offer our knowledge by way of mouth. We wait for the learning to come. If it is present a voice of understanding will emit from the one who offered a glimmer of hope. We have learned many have tried to accept this offered faith, but they have partaken for it simply to gain a new friend, something important but not the main reason for searching in the light. If value comes, we implement more by way of speaking in a cordial manner. If it is shot away, we forget the stand and watch for more leading. God, will at times, shut the doorway we are hoping to enter and guide us to a different area of the workforce. There is never a day without some event for us to watch and learn by. We realize man is fallible and in need of guiding, so we entertain in a discreet way. Not all who appear to have the light truly do so we must not act in haste, or we would lose our lives in a quick manner. The light must reside in a clear fashion and no lead of darkness should come forward. If an invitation of darkness presents, we know God is not the one making the introduction. We watch and invest only when presented with unity, so it requires standing in the way of Jesus' path for unity to be present. God is righteous and holy. In Him we have a bounty necessary to commit to the love we find. We think only as to how to share the love of the One so willing to offer hope. He alone is the care partner we blend to. Jesus is the way to survive in this time era and in Him is the light for man to be given unity. Without Him we are all doomed to death. Glory is His making.

God is the one who made my heart believe and in doing this great accomplishment I am now hope filled. I have gained many who seem interested in what I represent. I do not, however, open my thoughts with no influence from God. He operates so I am safe and in good standing with the government, but this will not always be. I have seen enough to envision that my time here is going to end. I will have to make a decision of where to flee due to the harsh reality no other is vital to the devil. He sends many before my path knowing I have the offered hope to invest toward others. He hates I can realize who is with him and who has the covering of God's armor upon them. Little suggestions happen and I understand when they are false by the way they are given. My heart sees the barrier of death and retreats from it. I have never witnessed a murder, but I hear of them daily. It is a harsh reality we must endure. The people I have a connection to know we must act with unity, or we will perish. It is in the unity God offers us that the understanding of who is sharing Him in their spirit is revealed. God is truly a love of hope and a call of wise trust. In Him I find the ability to work and gain instruction with support. I invest where I find the faith being shared and this is in the eye of the One who made us His own. Why would someone choose outside of light I cannot visualize? I have never invited deception into me. It has never been a goal for me to have something without understanding it is either from the Lord or it is from Satan. I have been deceived into thinking I could outwit the enemy, but I learned that is foolish thinking. He has the way of deception, and none can gain from his outreach. I shall not witness for him due to his presence being repulsive to me. I have found the One who matters and that is my Lord and Savior. In His view point I am more than a silly individual with no value. He has placed His arm upon my waist and together we walk as one with purpose. The love of the One who is so good never ceases to gain me in the way of unity. I apply my heart in His direct line of sight and good flows forth. How can I ever praise Him enough for His gift of me to Him? I value His manner and I work for Him these days not my bank account. I support my God and I gain from Him with every hope and idea for He maintains me with character. How am I to find anything greater? I don't even try for I know He is all things right and true. No other has this within him.

My offer is to stand with unity to the One I love and have value to. God is the gateway for me to know a personal blessing of insight. The unity I share is from on high. In the path of justice comes the unity man is in need of having. God supports my mind and in Him I have unity. To love the One of grace is far better than all things of value for He is superior to any other shield. I look in the mirror and see a light that didn't used to reside. I have now captured the undertaking of a math goal I couldn't deliver on my own merit. God is the source of my heart being a lighted goal. It is not my own undertaking for I am not that skilled. God is the one who had the knowledge of when I would act and come forth to Him. He invited me to share this knowledge and I freely bring forward His favor. God is the witness I believe and find rewarding. I have the goal of knowing where to find Him as He entertains me regularly within my heart. He speaks and I gain in the way of favor. He is not critical nor is He always correcting my every move. He works with the presence of care not just force. To know God is a stand of significant leading. He will show you where to send your idea making and how to spread His witness to others. It will be a plan of work that succeeds with character and good harmony. He will not place you in a situation you are not comforted by. If change happens and you determine it is of value work with the goal and see how God offers, it to you. I have gained the connection to my own ability due to His beautiful way of presenting me unity. I love our stand of leading and I am glued to Him with character. I reflect on how dark it used to be and I appreciate the love of God all the more. The trust I have placed within far exceeds the dark around me. I have value and I know I care for others in the same manner. God has supported me, and I thank Him for His courage through me. Today I send you this message. It is a gift of trust I gained from the will of God to my person, a quiet expression and gold to the heart.

7 For the Lord is righteous, he loves justice; upright men will see his face. Psalm 12:7 NIV

I have the truth to give and in me I have support so I know I can bend forth for another to learn by my witness. I am weak and in fear but the One who made heaven and earth stands as my defender. I know it takes courage to offer others value as we are not permitted to entertain this activity. I open my idea making in the form of a quick nod or smile; yet; at times others have done the same. We do not express anything beyond this but we look at one another in a caring way. Our eye expression is deep and with character. The love is seen and viewed by the spirit not just the visualization. We have the goal of standing for Christ and we want the rest of our workplace to find this hope. Many however, lean toward the dark one and believe in his way of life. We pray in the spirit when one of the innocent is sent to the gallows. We know it takes courage to withstand the whipping and chains. Paul from Scripture had to face such harsh responses from the civilized community he was party to. God, however, operates in a different manner. With Him there is peace and good favor. He is not one to force His idea of living onto anyone not interested in being His love child. I have the knowledge we are going to have to take forward the idea to a new location. Where will this be I am not sure, but I believe the Father will guide us when the time is at hand. I invest in goal building, so I pray with unity to secure the role I am to abide in. I love being cared for in the way of connection that leads with hope not devastation. In the way of knowing where to obtain the ability it simply happened when Christ came into me with trust. I have the way of being a silent being but with God I now operate so others learn and thrive. It takes a stand of insight for one to have the ability to offer to another the love God has but the provision is always available. Unity is what makes me comforted. The truth is what I accept, and it makes me a witness of bearing so I can operate in the way of good faith. God builds for me open pathways and I agree with His goal, so I never exceed my own understanding. I would rather have the unity to Christ than the freedom to stand alone. It is far better with a partner of light than no witness of community.

    The love of the One who made me is never ceasing to provide fruit to my heart. I have the value system of learning with character and a wholesome way. God has gifted me the instruction, so I share what I have to others in need. It comes by way of simple knowledge, yet it is endearing just the same. To understand the character of Christ is such a talent none can compare. He alone crafts the spirit and in Him is the sight I need to survive. The reason I invest is God is greater than all of mankind. He feeds me hope where others have failed. In the way of truth, He garners my mind in a clear and orderly way. Knowing the truth has given me protective qualities and I find I am at ease even at work. No one has offered me more protection and I thank the Savior for His faithfulness. To know the craft, I have begun is to stand in the manner of faith. It is what holds the heart of me to God. In the way of a committed partner, I lean forth to another for his hope to be gifted. I cannot do it for anyone, but I can offer prayer and leading, so they find God due to my offered instruction. I speak only to the ones who have the knowledge God is true and righteous. No people in front of me offer light. At my desk I see some gain a look, but none have offered me a hope in they have understood what it meant. They are silent but what I know may happen is one will unite against the offered love and call me a traitor. If this is to be my death, I will know God used me till it happens. I have the role of knowing many who have found the value of the outreach, so I am committed to stand on behalf of the One who gave me insight. He is precious to my heart so I shall not cry foul. In Him is the unity necessary to thrive, even if it is in this time era. So many have lost the benefit of God and have gone into the dark because they felt the desire to it. If one is not united to black heart ideas, he does not join in it. I have the message of favor and I share it with true hope. To accept defeat would just be a weak unity and God has given me much more resilience than I expected. Together we tie man's heart to the saving ability of God and in the plan comes the witness God is genuine with character and good leading.

    God, the Father of my heart, is the witness I lean toward for all faith. I have the heart of much favor due to His belief in my person. I am not the goal, but I can lead another where to find it. The passion I now entail is for all to find the unity of Christ before death arrives and tears away all hope for eternal gain. Knowing I have the light is a way of truth I have invested in. I accept God makes the trust build but by staying committed to expressive notes of hope I find many are tying their own favor to God. I look at where I used to be and find that today's way of being is far better than the stand of no unity. In God is the way I have always longed to be gifted. I just hadn't the unity till the joyous commitment happened. I took it to the line and then turned full attention to the One who called my heart His own. I invested with prayer and now I have the spiritual guiding to make a daybreak moment happen for another. To see a witness come forth gives me courage to continue to offer smiles and gestures of light. Where it is maintained, I continue but if no response is given, I wait for the goal to be made viable. Some have the born ability to express light in simple forms but not the whole countenance of it. It is verified in the way they stand in their share growth. If one is after a role of more wealth, it is quickly understood, and I pass off the knowledge. I do not attempt to force another to learn the lighted pathway. It can't happen without the heart of the person being willing to come to the saving power of Jesus. To surrender seems as defined as losing; yet, with God the Almighty it means a whole new birth takes place. How is this possible? Only the King can offer this knowledge and He conceals it for the time being. I do not have the stand to make a way for the dark thought process to thrive. I have never engaged in ritualistic behavior for fear of losing self-control. When God draws a person to Him the faculties are always maintained. One doesn't lose focus or standing. I learned the difference when the man of death claims his victims. One by one they have fallen and died, and this means there is no life within them for all eternity. What a sad way of ending one's life.

To know the One who made all the stars is a glory of hope I have vested within. I stand in the harmony of faith and in the care of me to others I spread the love forward. God has a purpose for me, and it is good. I never doubt I am making a difference but at times I feel small and insignificant. That is when I turn to prayer and lean into the Lord of life. The unity returns and I have the will to carry forward. The value of trust I have is due to the One who made me a witness to Him. There are those who have no insight, and they are leading in a false way. None of them talk in a favoring way and they all sleep together with no arrangement of unity for it all speaks to death. Disease is rampant and they don't even seem to notice the decay they have. Knowing the support of God guarantees, I realize the way ahead. In Him is the love of the nourishment necessary to offer hope and a stand of courage. God is true to His ability, and I have the way to work without having to offer my body to others. I pretend to have no value in it and look blankly at them when an invite comes to me. I never dress in a revealing way, so I do not tempt others who lack self-control. I remember when it was a game to entice the male counterpart into a look my way, but now I want no attention given to me. The men in the workplace relate to the many who freely give their character freedom in slavery for that is what truly transpires. The love of God is for man to save his gift of flesh for the commitment of marriage and the unity it provides. To love another without engaging in the act of matrimony means a true value is placed upon it. I have understood I can obtain a goal of entanglement with no clause. But first I would have to sacrifice my own pure way for it to happen and that is something I do not wish to ascribe to. I work because of the mandate but I would leave here if it were permitted. I now have plenty of wealth to live as a retiree due to the long hours and scripted way of no spending. I am not elderly but rather of an age of youth. In the pure heart resides the insight so I have gained the knowledge I am with the Lord in the decision of staying pure before Him.

My labor has the means of no value and I divulge no effort beyond that of the mandatory way of the work shift. I am not the one who works after hours and there is no reward to do so. Those who lead have lost the unity of self-goal making and have turned their hearts and minds toward the liar. The image of me has faded from youth and beauty is to a less important stand. I do not desire to have recognition for I would only have to surrender to the office predators. I work incognito and keep my head down so as not to have eye contact for even that stands out as witness making. But when a spirit in need presents, I know where to turn my focus and doors open. I then acknowledge it with a quick glance and the unity develops. If no support happens, I know the intent has risen to pure negative outreach. The unity God showers my way is proof He is real and great. Even the slightest nod supports my knowing attribute of the spirit. This I have learned is spiritual and not of the flesh. I have the ability to garner the hope and stand with another in their outreach to God. I pray and offer a slight turn in His direction. It is a simple gesture, but it comes forward with great support. The witness never leaves a person, and he begins to accept my offer if beauty is within. A gentle nod allows a cast of hope and in doing this act I am given the sight of a new soul being birthed. When the rejection takes place, I lose the connected response and I must then reject further offerings from the person. I don't know how this takes root within me, but it definitely transpires so I am assured of aid from on high. God has supported me with faith, and I stand with character waiting for the completion of the salvation process. When the goal is received, a spark is ignited and we bond in a quick manner. Otherwise, no response happens, and I reject the expression. Should I feel responsible for the one who fades into the black? No, for God is the one all man needs and if He is not welcomed, then neither am I.

God has the benefit of knowing who is for Him and who isn't. I learn from His witness to me how to accommodate the spiritual one who truly wants the Savior and His way of being. Together, God and I offer a united gift of support. Right now, there is little I can do but smile and host the heart due to the way of this age, but I still realize it matters. The all-knowing Christ is the one who made me and in doing this He crafted my heart to hear Him in perfect harmony. At times I wonder if I have the witness correct and if this happens, I wait for confirmation. If there is a tie of hope, I lean forward and develop the bond. God ordains who will meet my mark of love, so I know I don't have to stand alone without insight. Leading is a sight birth the King has offered me. The love and care of our unity is something I will always have value in. The love of the Maker is for all who believe and have the instilled gift of sight. To value the God of all mankind is to realize He is the one all need for hope eternal. I have no knowledge without Him, and I desire nothing more than to be in His care for it is good and holy. The unity far impresses to me the better path, so I invest in the way of it. The work of the saving grace is all I dream of having for God is this beacon of dream making. I know I am tied to God due to the safety plan He has offered. It is not that of any light but rather pure goal setting and honor. Without the love of God, I would have gone into a depression and lost the hope I now carry. Leading is for the way of God to mankind not man to Christ. The day of seeking another has dissipated and the unity I have supports me more than I am able to comprehend. I know God is far above my knowledge. And in the undertaking of sharing Him, little escapes me not right and favoring. Nothing of the darkness holds value. Not even the gift of wealth for it is a lie to the spirit.

The Father of mankind is not the one who offers support in a simple way for He possesses the unity we need for the life of eternal good. In Him is the birth of a unity leading to all things right and good. We, ourselves, are not capable of leading so others gain freedom of hope. It is only the power of Jesus that puts in motion our hearts to His way of being. In the way of a gift of favor man negates the role but where God's favoring all find the faith within. The light of the heart is a kindred response noteworthy of trust and kind leading. God is the way to find the love of His power to many. The man who develops the faith is not a simpleton but rather a strong influence of faith due to the revelation of support from on high. The way to adorn the breath of the Savior is to invite Him within the heart. It matters where you apply your instruction. God is the caretaker who never fails due to His ability to always be a witness of support. The leading and unity are tied, and the faith comes where man invests in the caretaking to another. It seems to be all who find God visualize a way to share Him in respect to what they have gained. If you are committed to learning the Word God administers to the heart and mind the reading gift to gain. The spiritual Being of hope is the trust favor of true honor. God does not offer a false support but one of insight and knowledge. To evolve without the process of true committed meaning man flounders and loses his way. The One who maintains the heart is God not mankind or his demeanor. Even the brave have no faith, if God is not the focal point in their idea making. The Lord carries the mind to the heart of His being and in doing this a record of unity is supported. To template to gain is for man to have the ability to regain his love in the manner of unity and care. Following a sacrifice man, feels he must then act in accordance with the offered degree of tied endurance but where God favors the support a gown of strength is cast toward the heart. The trust of the King is not a less than value but one of true insight. The necessary way to align the heart to Christ is to take responsibility and gift God the heart in a free manor. Leading is always that of intent with character if God is viewed with a garnering of truth. The leadership of the unity is for Christ to advance the support and tie the way to future ownership and truth. Never is the plan for man to have a loss or no pathway but in due time all fields of hope abound.

God instructs the heart and the notion of knowing Him it is fed. To give the body to the purpose of another is not how the true love of God is gained. Marriage to a person stands as an example of light and hope not disrespect of labor. In the marriage of a group light is abundant. This happens in a spiritual way not that of the physical. To own the part of you that breeds favor is to disqualify the heart from the connected lead of the Savior. God is all-knowing and in Him is the sight of trust leading to purpose. The care of many comes into play where another has the ability to gain for the sake of the group. This is community at work. True gain is not in the pocketbook, but it is a form of trust if God provided the goal, and it was seen as worthy of Him. Many believe work must be redundant when in actuality it needn't be. If you are having a difficult time with the standby way of your career you are in the wrong profession. Today, we aren't given the option to work in where we are fulfilled. Work placement is indentured not sought after. We no longer are given roles we enjoy as this is considered out of the way of future growth. Where man has the accomplishment of faith, he can withstand any burden man applies to him. But when God has the slate of our mind He provides us with a way to offer the field of study without loss and work becomes a labor of love.

God is faith in the way of capital to our heart. We unify with His stand and our ideas become better for it. The value of Him increases and we learn how to tabulate the honor of His counsel and true meaning follows our hearts. The love of Christ is not a gesture without hope, but it does mean we must pursue Him with favor. To pray and lead comes with intent, and this is the way to stand in the unity with the One who made you. The will of sharing the lead is a gain where we involve the favor of Him and seek his moral way. To offer this to others is not easy now but I do have the knowledge I am working for many even though it may not seem as though I am. Near the doorway of the office, I hear who is seeking to lead by way of faith and not that of just wealth which is for the account practice. I know who is maintaining the ritual for self and who is working due to having to lead even though they are not hoping for advancement. God features the heart revenue that is far better than money could ever be. If the value of the dollar is what is clearly being offered and a person rejects it, I know there is more to him than just the way of the government. I then seek to align with his person in the way of support with a note of hope and then I wait for a reaction. If it is seen as good, I know that individual hasn't lost himself in the dark. I attempt to offer a better path through the knowledge of unity and wait upon God to lead us together. The love of God is for those who lean into the work of God. When this happens, I know I have met another in the way of Christ. It is not difficult to hear who means to share the light and who is simply pretending. Their speech is unique and their way of being is bright. Even if the work is difficult, they don't complain. They stand at the station and offer their ability, so the workload isn't as harsh for another. It is witnessed but not so much so others complain. If the value of God is within them, we join in the heart. It is beautiful and good when it takes form. The one who made the first attempt is the one who is the guarantee of the connection. We speak in secret and operate with structure. We aren't wild in our outreach. It would be foolish to be so bold. God operates with a goal of sharing not force. So, in this same way we entertain the committed way of Him.

God is favor to the one who believes and invites Him to His way of being. The manner of Jesus is for the unity to be achieved. The most valuable unity is the tie to the Savior and Him alone. All examples of hope are simply Him in action. The faith of a mustard seed brings a way of trust none can compare to. How does this align with the will of God to man? It stands as the way to acknowledge Him with fruit and love. He divests the manner and gains the spirit the will of Him to grant the heart a better pathway. In the doing of this activity man learns where to accept the sight of God and to offer it to others. I work in this day of darkness without the unity of people, but God is the one who keeps me sustained. I have the offered goal of leading so others can achieve what I have found. Will I continue to claim the way of hope? It shall always be. My root is deep today, and I know I am not going to collapse in a heap on the floor of loss. I will always find a reason to carry forward the favor of God. Even if this is a stand in where all I have now washes away in labor alone. God will not abandon me, and He will offer me the sight plan to sustain my goal making. How He maintains me is done with the unity of Him not my own ability. He is the great one, all achieve to learn from. Even the person who has little knowledge finds the process a calm insight. But the one who dreams of only ash examples falls into despair. The love God provides is a clear incentive driving man to the light. God knows what is necessary for a person to invite Him into his spirit. Some come with a fuel for the long haul and then they lose interest. Others find the support and it turns to a negative within them. Yet, there are the ones who offer their whole being to God and they stand for the duration of the length of the witness. They are coupled in matrimony to Christ. This is the way of the faith bearing people of light. To believe in the One who offered His heart and body so man could know the Father in a complete way is the same influence calling in your heart today. If you are hoping to have a different unity, you have no ability to find it for this is the master's plan of salvation. It is far more identified by the love of God than by man's own aid to himself. People who find the faith to be that of a complete trust are a witness in they support God and offer to Him the love and care to others just as He would. How did I learn such news? God provided me the understanding in the way of saving ability from the moment I accepted Him. He has taught me where to place my heart and how to find the proof of His faith by working with the unity of me to His counsel. I believe He has showered me with trust, and I have invited Him completely to rule my every thought. I do not desire to work outside His character. He leads with such hope I yearn for more of His outreach to me. I never realized until I claimed Him that it would be such a good experience day in and day out. The one who doesn't find this union has not truly loved God or cared for Him in a significant way. The difference in me is what I lean into when I feel weak or afraid. It reminds me Christ saved me as His one and only never to step away from me or force me to aspire to His way. I come with an open manner to offer myself in a way of trust that exceeds my own understanding. I do not leave empty-handed as He grants me the way ahead with clear light. I shall always have the knowledge God is all supportive to me. I value the One who places me in such high esteem.

    Christ is my forever hope and light. I do not fear what lies ahead though within me is a loss when I think of the many yet missing. I know I will see them again but until that time I am without their presence. God is my all in all; yet, man needs a partner in the way of fellowship to mankind. We are designed to offer our insight and the glory of God comes into play where we knit as a team of faith builders. The love of the One who made my goals so complete is ever with me in character. I have the will of the scout who looks for opportunity and in the way of knowing where to align myself to another. I have the witness I long to share in the right path leading others to the heart of the King. To know the One I favor is to align with His person. I have the sight of knowing who is thinking about faith and where to apply it but I still long for conversation regarding the Maker. To have the knowledge without the expression is not what I invest toward. Little steps are all I can advance in, yet this is where God has placed me for the time era I stand upon. The role of care is for the one who sees a need and acts forward to share the light. God is ever on the move. He operates with the goal of building so many find the support of Him as their own witness. Leading so another is accepted into the fold is what my heart engages in. I pray with insight and hope due to the love of God before me. The way I gain a stand is when God the Father opens the door for me to gift to another the hope of Jesus. It appears this is to be in a quiet fashion but nonetheless it is valued.

The love of God is to me in a unique way for I am one of His witnesses. He uses me to offer hope in the dark. I stand in support of knowing the great I Am and in this insight, I offer to mankind the knowledge I gain. He has made me secure in the knowledge He aspires to teach through my offered unity. He will not fail in this commitment. I savor the will of His caring way and in knowing Him I alone receive the benefit. However, to many I teach the same care I have been gifted. The will of God is for me to align with Him in the manner of true hope, so I never feel amiss in my insight. I believe He can obtain within my mind the way to operate and where to lead from. God is not one to cause me harm or loss. In Him I have the gain of being a fellow faith lead that abides with the character of the Living Word. He offers me the better path even in this time and era of darkness. How do I stand when there is little remaining that speaks of light? It is by the will of Christ I lean into Him for the unity. I have the ability to stand without Him, but this would be foolish to invest in. I realize He is the reason I breathe air and that none have discovered me. Today, I have the heart of a person who believes in the option of knowing the One who made me with the goal of faith I now hold. It came due to placing my heart toward the true way of insight. I now have another hope to release. It came in the night, and I invested in the memorization of it so others could hear it too.

I am a Scared Witness

1 Now faith is being sure of what we hope for and certain of what we do not see. 2 This is what the ancients were commended for. 3 By faith we understand that the universe was formed at God's command, so that what is seen was not made out of what was visible. Hebrews 11:1-3 NIV

The Word of Christ is all I know that means light. Even though I hear the voice of God at times it is not always Him speaking. The enemy desires for me to lose my way and fail in the knowledge God is real. I work with support from God, but I also know I need to stand in caution when I am building the work before me. I believe I can lose my heart if I don't apply the Word of the Living God to my person. I must adhere to the love of Christ and pray with unity. I know the enemy works against my heart and in him is hate and lies. I think about the lost and how they have no unity to the great I Am. It makes for a loss within my spirit but to offer all the light would go against the mission I have been given. I must wait upon God to gift me the ones who will offer their will to the King. It takes patience and love and due to the offered way, I must lean into God for security and a stand of strength. All the people I have known as favored are now in a different sight birth of faith. We connect and work together so others find the unity we have favored. Light is not the mission but rather to know the God of mankind. He is the gift of salvation and in Him is our stand of gain.

God is true and good. In Him is light with character and a framing of hope. I never leave the comfort of Him for He stands within me. I value His counsel and I accept Him for the One of glory. To know Him is a gain none can compare with. I love knowing I have such comfort and holy standing. I am a sinner but still I have been redeemed. How this came to be, was the profession I need a Savior. I asked for forgiveness, and I was claimed by Him. He never asked me to offer blood or stated I was insignificant. The power of the One who made all things good is within my heart and I am given unity. By the declaration of faith, I gained the moral code of love. It was by this witness I learned to repent and seek forgiveness of my sins. I was washed in the blood of the Lamb, and I came to an understanding I am now whole. I did not rush to Him with my own being but rather He came to me in my time of need. I knew He called, and I heard Him. I now know I could have had Him before this horrific time frame, but due to my own selfish ideas I am now here standing in the midst of loss. I never had the courage to offer others my learned way until He intended for me to learn the value of His nature. It happened the moment I invited Him to my person. The trust it took was simplistic; yet, all-encompassed. I now reside with unity and caregiving and they matter to me like my own heartbeat. I am not one to call others unworthy for all of mankind is valued by God. I have the gift of prophesy and within this unity I know who is willing to invite God to their hearts and minds. It took the accepting of the One called Savior for me to act in such a manner. Before this I only envisioned my own unity. I did not believe I was important to another's care.

The creation of my heart is not what matters most to the Lord. It is my belief and my hope toward Him. I now have the plan of a witness in love, and I share this knowledge where able. At times I still tremble and lose my thought process, but God assures me once more I am valued. This stands as the marker for me to continue to work for the saving power of God to others. If fear settles in, I know the enemy is laboring to affect my witness. I pray and find the courage from God. To review the many passages I know and recite, gifts me the favor needed to invite another to the love of the One of grace. The light and knowing ability of the Caretaker is solid and informative. In Him is the way to have prosperity. Even though our time is wasted performing on the market of only wealth due to the law we administer a value just the same. We ignite the plan of favor by applying our hearts in the direction of a real standing. God is the one who shows us where to place our value and it is always right and good. The gift of study I now complete is a detailed description of faith. I have learned the Word by Christ and memorization, and I tell another what I gain. The truth of the Word has settled my heart, and it offers me value beyond measure. The ability to learn in this way has come as a surprise to me. I never used to retain like I do in this arena. I believe God has proven Himself righteous in I have such a love for the retention of His way. I value to learn the Scriptures by way of applying what I know to another. God sends to me the one in need and I lean forward with care to him. It takes little to be understood in that none here do this. It is not for the faint of heart as it could mean the end of my witness. Time has presented several who needed the final goal to be heard and that took place by my individual belief impressed in prayer toward them. It seems so grand to be a part of the mission field; yet; I know it is not by my own witness but by that of God the spirit. He alone is the one who ordains who is sent to me. I have no offered knowledge about the faith just the message to give. To have the will and care of unity is what I gift and in doing this action others learn the work of God is precious.

God is the way to survive in such a time as this. Without His support I would have lost all value and become a human with no hope or insight. Due to the love and care God has to me I survive with true hope and leading. It is a value I do not lose when I offer it forward. Sharing is a state of support I needed to offer grace and insight of faith. When a person shares his skill, others learn and growth occurs. God shows His favor when one applies forward His learned knowledge. I used to think people would steal my thoughts and make money of their own and not gift it to me back but now I know this is foolish thinking. No two people are the same at what they do. Some thrive with the birthing and others have no notion how to perform the feat; yet, the one who applies his heart and mind forward to gain the unity finds the trust was well placed. The lead of the King is for man to offer his understanding in the way of a spiritual finding. It means to share your heart and trust others to do the same. Many today only take without offering anything in return but this only confirms the Lord's unity to me. I am not one to offer my hard-earned paycheck but leading the bounty to someone who has no home stands as a witness God is alive. I do this without it being detected. I have the value of knowing other's accounts, so it leads to being able to offer others some intelligent gain by way of leading in the banking system. The person I am guided to is a light beam where others are simply standing in loss. If the value of God is being presented, I know we are one to another in faith. We work where there is the hope and in doing this measure others see kindness. The beauty is something given in a secret way, not out in the open. I enjoy I can connect with the necessary bounty and reward another with support, some kindness and unity to guide the need and an offered stand in the way of favor. God is the one who gifts me this skill and it took time for me to comprehend this. I used to think if I applied my heart and work life to the goal of mastering the reward of a degree, I would be able to have wealth and savings. Today, I realize I only had the idea of unity not the understanding of it. The truth of my heart now resides with character and favor due to God's hand upon it. I am valued!

God has the prosperity of knowing where to find the one who is in need. He permits me to offer the faith I know is real. I guard my heart and wait for the signal from on high. It comes to me in where the heart hears the voice of Christ. It never tears me from the love I have, nor does it witness to me a loss in the ministering to another. The heart sees where the mind cannot. I know the One of all is at work administering to me the ability to offer a lead so another can grow. I look to the way of being placed in the knowing path of support. The care is always within my person, so I kneel in value to God. I have the offered truth and I learn from God where to tread. Leading means: To have the knowing ability to accept when no other is vested and to wait for the timing of God to happen. The leading is defined in I now receive the necessary guiding of unity to mankind. It happens where the heart is actively invested in the search of Christ. If a person speaks to me in such a way that light is born, I know he is committed to knowing the One who made him. The unity is then aligned, and we connect with hope. I never lead in the way of stepping into the fire of no known way for it would lead to no hope being planted. People are watching and I must be careful who I engage my heart toward. Lies spread quickly and even if I haven't bent the rules I may be accused if I act in a holy way. I stand in the silent way of prayer with no words said aloud. It would be a gift to pray with someone who knows the Savior but today we must keep this private. We hear our hearts connect so we know when another is being prayed for. The ability is not hard to accept. It came with the recognition God is the one who maintains our hearts. I have the gift of knowing where one of the sight-bearing people resides due to the address displayed on my computer. I am in the fog of doubt when I do not seek the wise words of God. I remember to apply my heart to Him then the clear unity is gained. I have the unity I need to accept His support when He places before me someone in need. I know I am to advance in the path of leading and I entertain this will with courage. God, the Father, is good and right. In Him is the character of sainthood. He is more than a price of hope for he alone cared enough to offer His Son to the people of the world for the sake of knowing Him in a personal relationship. What a precious hope He portrayed! To love mankind so deeply the relationship was valued above death was an intention of good harmony we must bind to. Leading in this knowledge is a care package I will always invest in.

Sight is a gift where man is fed and supported due to the acceptance of Jesus before him. God is perfect and in Him is the value of life. The favor of the One who made man is the offered sight all of mankind needs. To know the One of light is to reflect Him with unity. I invest due to the call He put before me. It was not known to me until I embraced Him and believed in His witness. The salvation of man is due to God being the way of eternal gain. To know Him is better than anything living or dead here on this planet. There is no reason to believe He is not who He claims to be for the Book of hope shares the knowledge and a record of all the unity He placed is mentioned. I have gained many verses and now I plant them to others by way of sharing them in a verbal correspondence. The door for this stands with hope but the goal is to share where able. I can't simply put it on the web as I would be carted off to training camp or shot and hung in the street. I know to offer another this unity is a bold framework, but I am compelled to do so just the same. Knowing God is far better than keeping Him within me without reaching out to others in need. The people streaming past my workstation have no idea I can understand their intent. Some try to make conversation who are working for the enemy but I don't engage. I hear them but I do not respond. The blackness of their minds is a stand I stay clear of knowing they cannot be reached until they invite God in and His way. This may not be the thing they hope to value so I wait for the bond of sight to be revealed. Many today are working in the way of sharing the sight we gained. It happens with subtle stands and offered hope. We take no action until someone comes spiritually with value to God. We know the one who is pretending so we refrain from that person.

God, the all-knowing King of hope, is planting my image within Him. He hears my goal making and knows I stand in support of Him. The unity to His heart is solid and I have the faith I can bring others to Him in character. Tonight, I gained another investment in the grouping of Scripture. It is a sign to me I have enabled others to learn as well. The gift is secure within my heart and mind for I have learned it and memorized it for my own intake and that of another.

6 Be strong and courageous. Do not be afraid or terrified because of them, for the LORD your God goes with you; he will never leave you nor forsake you." Deuteronomy 31:6 NIV

Robin (Rochel) Arne

4

Light is Difficult to Find

The workplace is not a secure place of hope. I must gift no heart gain until the Lord has shown me who to blend in harmony toward. It takes patience and unity to God to stand where no breath is in sight. To know the people of my station, have no intent of being one of the faithful is a sight that is hard to endure. Loss is everywhere and no other than God sustains me. I know He keeps me in His care, but it is difficult to hear of the many that have lost their lives due to courage for God. It is hard being one of them and not administering support at the time of death. To know I have never gone to a death sentencing would stir the people and cause misgiving ideas to come to light. I must stand where I am currently placed and believe God, the one of courage, has this under His wing of goodness. The all-knowing Being of unity does not fail nor will He. The little I am able to perform on behalf of the saving power I now contain is at times a feeling of little support, but the truth is far from this. I know I have witnessed unto many who have come before me. I stand on this promise, and I lean into it for support. I am not the saving power, but I hold it within me. God alone is the great one of light. He is the Master of dream building. He aligns the heart and maintains the spirit with truth. Without the love of God, I would have caved and gotten the mark of the enemy being damned for eternity. What a fate of defeat that would have been. I may reside where it is difficult with little light bearing but there is the unity I crave being fulfilled. The offer of favor has been within me, and I gained the support needed to offer others the truth. I am ever grateful for this gift. To lead in the way of faith has supported me with trust. It has built within my heart the goal of maintaining many so God can claim them with His love. Knowing God draws man to Him is a stand I have incorporated since learning of His goodness. To lead the many who are intertwined with character feeds my trust and I know I am being used. The date of my demise may come but in the meantime, I will engage where I am able. The light of the Savior far surpasses my inabilities, so I know every approach of harmony to mankind bears witness to the way of His presence. The love and character of Christ is what feeds me with righteous fruit. Never do I intend to ever stray.

I am safe in the arms of God with support leading to peace so where would I go to gain this acknowledgement. There is no other place as justified or good. Training comes by way of the unity and in the making of my heart I am fed trust. It sustains my mind over that of fear. I walk with the faith of a mustard seed, and I intertwine my faith with the many who have invested in the care of me with their heart. I hear them speak and encourage my offering of hope. Together we unite and walk by the administering of unity found in the plan of salvation. We grow and learn where to administer love and we offer it to any who claim the Lord as their eternal Waymaker. Glory to God on high for He is good!

20 He replied, "Because you have so little faith. I tell you the truth, if you have faith as small as a mustard seed, you can say to this mountain, 'Move from here to there and it will move. Nothing will be impossible for you." Matthew 17:20 NIV

Jesus knew when to call and I heard Him with a clear faith. You, as well, can learn and develop from His hand. I now have little opportunity to invite the love of God to others but still I manage to care and offer light. God has given me the way and in this gift I stand in the gulf of light. The people who have been insightful for my knowledge have gone forward to place the knowledge to others who came in view. At work I have the light due to reading Scripture God has offered me through visionary support. I know I have the stand of unity due to this enlightenment. God supports the one who offers others what they learn. The value of the King is for all to learn from. God is unity and in Him is the gulf stream of trust. To yearn for love is natural, but if God is your focal point you have a partner none can compare to. Many have flush bank accounts and reside with the faith that it will keep them in good standing, but much cannot be obtained by a witness of cash. Leading so another has the concept of favor is to qualify them with unity to God. If you found a source of knowledge and have applied it to God's people, you can rest in the unity God will offer it to others. The will of mankind is to stand where the unity is found. In Jesus we have the same heart one to another, but it is in Him we thrive and flourish. The many who have found the unity also stand in a way of favor due to expressing the knowledge as character and leading. Not all endeavors produce a return. However, if you have the dream of a ministry, God knows the need of the material side and He won't build you without hope. In Him is the mutual way of entangling the relationship and true honor is gifted. God supports the person who invests and aligns himself to Christ. Jesus is the way to thrive and find faith. His value to you is what sets in motion the guiding way of light sending others to the care and outreach supportive to their mind. Knowing the God of man is to value Him and lean forth to His character.

God is faith and, in His way, we offer the knowledge of completeness. God is the one who ordains the heart and to see Him as holy is right and good. I have the unity needed to find faith in an accepting way due to the One who made me whole. I have the value of Christ and in the way of faith I am supported with character. The all-knowing Creator is my guidance counselor. He has vested me to gift to others the knowledge of a plan, so others find the faith as I have. How this comes to be is by His own making for I am not the favor of the spirit. It is God alone who is the gift to mankind. I am the guide as far as staying near to encourage and gift support. I do not claim the Risen God is not who made all of mankind for I know He has created me in His image. The trust I have is due to Him working in me and not outside my character. I have united to His spirit and in this I am given the understanding He is good. The knowledge of Christ far surpasses that of any man. No other can attend to all with a way of beauty at all times. God is unity and good harmony. His character feeds my spirit with goal making. Due to Him I am in the way of future growth in my work area. I do not engage without unity but where I see a need for a better lead, I offer my knowledge and show support. I have not sought a path where I advance as I have no desire to work longer hours, nor do I want to gain more in my bank account. We are still expected to maintain the role we have and in the promotion field one has to work as a manager and an employee. I have seen the harshness of leading in today's managed time frame and I realize it is not safe to aspire for more identification in the workplace.

27 So God created man in his own image, in the image of God he created him; male and female he created them. Genesis 1:27 NIV

The way to offer light is done in secret without direct giving. We hide our knowledge and lean forth so God can gift us the union of a partnered engagement. God is faith within the heart. It is by His way I know I am maintained. The unity is far reaching, and the love is all-encompassed. God is the path for me to pursue and I work for the better of another. I have the sight of knowing where to operate and how to invite a fellow patron into the care of God. It is simple unity not that of whole team making. God favors me with the open doors, and I walk through them with trust. If I fail to hear the voice of trust guide me to speak, I remain silent and wait to see where it leads. I do not push my way forth for there is no hope in doing this output. God is the one who knows the spirit and, in the offer, I must remain in His guidance. He is all-knowing not I. The unity I give is far more than a simple gesture for I hear the care of Christ through me, and this offers my heart the goal of more outreach. To know and learn as I lead is a gain none other has offered. It indicates once more God is the only way to thrive and find support. The love of the King is standing strong, and I know He operates in unity to many who have found Him supporting them in these dire conditions. The hope from God is what maintains me and sets my heart a flame. The significance of reading the Scriptures I have been given means I gain every time I place value to them. I have learned to contain my thought process, so I don't act too quickly and lose my security in the quiet offering from on high. It can be a challenge not to express my knowledge in a quick way as I desire for all to know God and to find Him trustworthy. The way I work is to align with God and He speaks to me in a private way. He is true to His counsel and in Him is the faith required to know He does not leave me without support. I must gift my knowledge where God leads and not run forward too hard and fast. God is order and a managed character. I remember this and I gain the faith of waiting in the quiet. God is all-knowing and He shows me where and how to invite the lost to Him. Anyone in need is reflected to my heart and then I watch where the hope builds.

God is unity to the refined spirit that invests and believes He is the Waymaker. To value the One of light is a path of trust that incorporates the heart to believe in a righteous way. God, the one who guides the mind, is all-knowing and holy. In Him is the gift of unity we need to survive in a free manner. It would seem for many God is not a stand of freedom but in actuality it is exactly what His makeup consists of. The One of hope is a guide in where man is fed the support of favor due to the love of Christ. In the way of feeding comes the outright love and care of a provider. God is the one who made heaven and earth so I know He can do far more than any other is capable of. To perfect the support, one must learn who makes the message a light beam of unity. God is that very being. He alone is the one to craft the will of our hearts into that of unity and standing. The armor of our mind is supported where it finds the love of God to be holy. God never changes nor does He request man to stand without unity. As a prayer partner, I have learned God works within my scope of trust. If I believe He will make a way for me to have a need met He then offers a plan, and it begins to form in a righteous way. When I fear the process, I lose the hope and must wait for God to refuel my heart. I gain when I place my trust within Him. I have the reward of hearing Him and the unity stands with character. God is the one who invests without a loss or harm. To gift Him with my own unity is to stand on His behalf and to apply my direct coordination to Him. The well house is His spirit and I have the benefit of finding care where He resides.

The offered trust is not all there is to the build of a goal. The steps must consist of a plan where all aligns, and growth occurs, not hardship. God knows the unity and how to bring it forth. He leads so man can abide with support to Him. The light and care God provides is a sheath of good healing for the soul that has been harmed. To know the One invested is to understand He operates where welcomed. In the making of a dream God manufactures the bounty. Even now I know I am given support in the way God brings the slightest of hope my way. The people I meet have little to comfort them and in offering a simple gesture they find support. God is perfect to the one who has the faith enough to adhere where the door remains shut. The progress is still in action. Hearts are being mended and minds are capturing the unity. God is a beam of structure tied to a frame of value. He is always working for the good of all. If value is on the table, know God will align Himself the knowing way of feeding others. Where there is support, God marks the ground with favor. The unity is in line with Him when doors of opportunity open and care is given. The saving ability is His alone, so I know I needn't fear who comes to Him or who walks away. I embrace the one who claims God for himself, and I share where the option is offered. Leading requires the heart to stand with confidence even if the goal is not in sight. Knowing God cares about your every need is symbolic to His character. He hears your heart and knows when you press forward in His way of leading.

God is significant to the many who have valued His lead. The time it takes to acquire this knowledge varies from person to person. Why is this the case? Man chooses to either press forth to God or he sustains his own way. In the course of study in Scripture man finds the growth and courage is gained. The one who develops the love of the King develops the way of Him. In doing this manner he begins to build for the sake of those around him and this is honoring to God. The value of man is for all to learn and gain the knowledge God is true and trustworthy. God is all-knowing and a way of being a light source. The unity of Him is a bond not that of little knowledge but rather bright and hope bearing for all. The value of knowing the God claimed presence is a right and hope filled bounty. God is not one to wake the current but rather He aligns the heart and offers it a path of patient walking. The unity of the Caregiver is far above that of one's own ability or making. To know the great Lord of all is to believe in Him as your guidance counselor. Many have tried to lead when no insight was before them. This is a loss in the way of operating. To know and believe in the saving power of God is a factor people lean toward. The bright way of God calls to the spirit and it either embraces it or turns to the darkness. There is a division between the two and the better way is to follow the hope of the light.

The life of man is for the trust of him to be garnered to Christ. In knowing the plan of salvation man finds the faith to offer this goal and unity to all who come his way. The value of it can't be determined but the beauty is witnessed. When a person believes and shares the upright stand of unity from on high great support is given. The will of any who invest in the way of faith lead with an expectation God is who He professes to be. If you share the love of the One who bought you with His blood, you have the knowledge God is superior to that of anyone. Following in favor is a sight and a unity in where the lead of trust is a sight plan for those who have the trust of Jesus. The One who made the ground you walk upon can make a seed bloom to a flower with ease. The manner of knowing the trust to God is not that of a failing tribute but one of holy sight preparing the heart for the day of salvation. If you find you are looking forward to seeing the One of hope you have the light within you. Those who do not aspire to be with the God of man have no inherent expectation God is supreme. Life in the care of the Word of God gifts us the true knowledge He is all that is good. To tally this, man must operate with character and true witness making. Even those having faith as small as the orange on a tree will in character and meaning build and grow. Favor is for the one who develops his role of leading due to the character of Jesus. The ability of the manner to him who believes has the sight of knowing where to align the mind. God has the spirit within to perfect His stand and our own trust is built due to the way of favor. Where the purchase is made to bring others to the heart of the Savior gain will be present. It may take time for this to happen but serve in the trial as a warrior of value to Him who made your heart invested.

The trust of the One who made you gains the heart the revenue needed to thrive. The faith of the Caretaker is spread to you when you believe and engage in support. To offer the love you have to the Father is to guarantee the heart knows his Creator. The meaning of faith is for the heart to hear and accept the light of Christ. He is the value needed to gain unity and knowledge flows from His person. If you have the heart and the will to grant others this truth, you will be given opportunities to do so. The value of this stand is capable of wielding a math equation none can compute for God is the sight of this hope. The One who made you is all-knowing, and He never loses His path. The way of favor is to offer it to those in where alignment is understood. How can this be? If you imbed your mind to the character of the Living Word, you find the trust builds and the heart engages with hope. God supports any idea of hope and in the making of the idea comes the plan and the ability. If you have the will to ordain the unity and the goal of care, support will blossom. The way to align your heart to God is to say He is the Waymaker for man to live in eternal gain. The One who maintains the heart is all-encompassed so He never fails in His work ethic. The unity and the support of the One who determines the path declares the where and when of the goal to be had. The way to offer another the trust of God is to pray and stand as a witness with favor as your backdrop. God moves so people claim Him as supportive. If time has evaporated trust your King to have the nourishment to maintain the faith. Moving in a swift manner will be a collapse of the mission. Where there is unity, all things combine to gain man the heart and witness of growth. God ordains where He is welcomed. Light the switch of favor and talk with hope to others. You will invest and true insight will happen. A dream or stand of new thought processes may be the change needed to offer a path in declaration. You have the honor of the Father to your person. Know He hears all your intent. When the offered hope stands in a continual manner look for a path to happen and align your hope to it. God is true to His offering so balance Him with unity. In the correct way light will appear and truth will engage the mind. Stand with support and know the manner of the favor of God is to conquer the darkness and make it pour forth with good knowledge.

    The time to connect is the moment you have where light is enduring and flowing forth. Where the honor of God is present favor is at work. The unity and the structure of the pairing is not one of little expectation. In the way of faith man needs to abide with the goal of knowing the righteous God of all. It is not a slim way to breathe in hope but rather a unified presence of trust. The One who maintains the heart can bring to it the love of Christ. God is the support beam necessary to offer the pattern of mileage in where a true sight is given. God has the will to carry the heart in the direction of worthy timing. If you have a gift of working for others to have a better way know God made you a witness to Him in this means. The perfect way of faith is a sight known as giftedness. God is spiritual and in His way of being the fruit of the favor abides. The love of Him is to care about every detail of a desire. In His gifted way He compliments the heart and favors it with truth. If you have the notion to build let God show you the plan. He is righteous and true and in Him is the gift of support. He will pave the trust with the means and in doing so you will prosper with unity. He does not fail in the mission of knowing your idea plan so wait for Him to determine where and how. It will reflect to you His stand and you will know Him as valued. The shadow of God casts light so trust Him with your whole being. This will be the wise investment you enjoy and receive.

I have the hope I will meet the Lord before the time of death. He is due to come again, and I wait with trust. I know I do not have all the understanding within me but I believe I am standing on His promise to claim His bride before the whole world implodes. God cares for mankind, and He stands in unity to his demeanor. I know the right offense is with the one who stood on Calvary's leading. God, the one who ordained mankind to have a better life witness, has also known man would fail in this endeavor. Where the support of the King comes forth is in the way of trust to the heart. God does not send His heart to the one who's only desire is that of wealth for there is no benefit with that mentality. The knowing determine God is all-encompassing and offers the same to mankind in that under His wing of holiness we are made righteous. I value the way of faith and I apply my hope in the direction of favor for it is the better way. Knowing the One who made me is to trust His lead and to ascribe to it with character. I know I have the witness of a woman in love with her Savior so others find me attractive. The level, playing field is found in the matrimony of God to me. I have not understood how to operate with only a signature stand but as the days pass by I realize it is enough to learn on a daily basis. God supports my love of Him and in this unity I tie to His grand manner. I have the will to conquer the world for His glory, but I am small and without the ability to do such a thing. Only the One of all-knowing knowledge can offer such standing. I am worth His attention as He gifts me this truth. He values man above all other creatures. In Him is the truth of Scripture and in the commitment of Him to my heart I gain respect.

1 As a prisoner for the Lord, then, I urge you to live a life worthy of the calling you have received. 2 Be completely humble and gentle; be patient, bearing with one another in love. 3 Make every effort to keep the unity of the Spirit through the bond of peace. Ephesians 4:1-3 NIV

God delivers where others are unwilling to offer unity. He is the one who develops the heart to work for the greater way of Him. To know the One who made you is a sight of standing others hope to achieve but without the knowledge of the written Book of hope man fails to thrive. God supports us with this character and in doing this favor we achieve goals of pure leading. Had the Savior been party to my life before this era, I would reside in complete bliss. But due to my own rejection I must wait in the dark of this time and pray for safety. I know I did not unite because I desired my own way; yet, God loved me through the loss and claimed me as His just the same. I know I have the ability to withstand the long era of draining, but I would rather have been safe with Him at my side. He now has me carefully hoisted to His person, but I must refrain from reflecting Him in a grand manner. I have the knowing ability He is ever near so that is comfort and security. To have the knowledge of Him is far better than no understanding but one must invest in the relationship and support Him with true love. I have the intent of sharing Him for I believe it stands as a witness I am valued. I live as though no other has heard of the One of great value, but I know that is not what is right. For God the mighty caregiver has many in His fold of people who have committed themselves to knowing Him and granting others this gift. I believe I have the gift of prophesy, and in this gain I can hear another's favor from on high. I look at the person God has shown to me, and I invite his delivery of hope to my own unity. We experience faith and it leads us to gain. God is good to me in this way, and I thank Him for the favor.

    The faith I put toward another is from the One who has a vested interest in my well-being. I am not alone in that God is ever within my heart. I yearn to be by Him but for now I must refrain from despair. I value the gift of instruction and in the way of the care He administers I have support. Knowing He is ever with me garners my heart in His direction and I have the faith leading to others finding Him good and harmonious to them. The light I have is found by way of tying my knowledge to His heart. It came to me while a confession of love was expressed. I believe I am always with hope due to the way He operates and who He is as a Lord of divine knowledge. The character of Him is total and complete and I never have to lose my own manner but in Him I favor His leading above that of my own offering. To know God is a way of life for me now. I never would have imagined I would be so infatuated with the One who made my heart but there is none better to know. I can almost hear Him on His stallion calling my name as He arrives in Jerusalem to save mankind from his own demise. The way of guarding my spirit is to call to God and offer Him my value. I know Jesus is all-knowing and He maintains my heart and all I cherish is His.

    The love of Him who gains to offer mankind the love He gives obtains a certain stand of unity. When God offers a goal, remain in the way of faith with the expectation He does not fail. God is perfect and true. When He guides a good matrimony is heard. God is all-powerful and in Him is the necessary guiding to perfect the will of Christ forward. God is the care one has, and in this stand of trust is a vital way of being. Harmony is fed due to the managed unity God is witness to. If you value your own way and step forth in the way of selfish ambition losses will ensue. Where God does the claiming goals are in line and hope is built. A gold offering may take the heart to a quick knowledge, but will it offer the full value as the first understanding? If no other aids the heart wait with support and build with prayer. Your idea will become a plan and there will be a guided light that outlines the spirit. Knowing the leading of God is not all there is to the unity. If you value His lordship, you will remain in His way of thinking. The light and harmony will engage with your thought process and trust will be abundant. Dark thoughts only bring a less coherent authority, and no real value is gifted. Change does happen but the knit way of the presence of God will capture your heart and you will ordain the gift with support. I have value due to my love of the Creator. He has led me to the place of structure that unifies my heart with Him. I accept I do not have all the answers and I cannot make a dream build without Christ. Where I sit is a tidy place with no infrastructure, but I have God's offered ability to reach forth and smile onto many who pass by. This may seem to be a small offering but where there is light, I proceed in character and gain a friend in need. The gift is strong, so I know it matters just as much as the One who made the goal align. No, no other is as important as God. What I am saying is the Creator has given me the heart of Him to share and it means I know Him in this way.

God factors all of man's initiatives and in His way of knowing who is righteous and who just pretends comes the knowledge of His power. The many who do not believe or stand in support of Him will not embrace Him when He returns. They will be lost to the way and have no hope within them. But they will bow the knee to Him at the Judgment Seat. God will stir the mind and make it correct and, in His counsel, man finds the favor needed to work for the truth of knowledge to be shared. If the value of God is far from your heart, you may not have the belief of Him within. The unity is more than a simple notation of God. It is a witness for His embodiment to flourish within your person. God delivers the knowledge by way of His spirit and the reading of His Word. The unity one gains far surpasses the dollar and the gold coin. God captures the mind and shadows it with favor. The realization God is all-knowing must be understood. The unity of God to mankind is a grant of gain negating the one who is evil. God is the right and fruitful love of the people. All have the unity available. What determines the way one thinks is whether he desires to have the witness of light upon his manner. The capturing of unity comes when the heart believes and accepts the truth God is the true Savior, not a simple idea of one. If there is a witness from your heart and mind and you offer it forward God is at work in your heart. His leading comes into play when He is given the means to bond with you in a personal way. God is not a secret for all know Him. It is the one who decides to pursue the Living God of creation who benefits from His spiritual guiding. The love of God to mankind is all- encompassed. The knowing way to proclaim the Lord is not due to the value alone but the whole bond of hope He portrays. Even the weak will stand in the light of God and not lose their life due to no feeding of the heart. A small inkling of God will sustain the person seeking to know Him for the power of Christ is rich with unity.

10 You, then, why do you judge your brother? Or why do you look down on your brother? For we will all stand before God's judgement seat. 11 It is written: "'As surely as I live, says the Lord, every knee will bow before me; every tongue will confess to God.'" 12 So then, each of us will give an account of himself to God. Romans 14:10-12 NIV

God is the material goodness of fruit of the heart. In Him man finds the support leading to a rich way of life. Money fades and in the manner of it so will your idea of having it as your only hope of gain. God knows who values Him above the money or fame. He has given man the wise stand of knowing how to pursue Him in faith. The one who places his heart in the palm of God gains the unity necessary to thrive in a world where others lose their trust. The commitment of God is always that of a true knowledge. He does not change, nor does He reinvent His way of being, so we never have to care for another above Him. God alone is the great Almighty. We do not lose standing by administering the light forward. It is a complete hope offered to any who believe and invite God to their person. God is the unity man desires and in doing the action of accepting Him we find the love He offers. The way of God is to care for all who invest toward His heart. Know God is not the one to leave your side. He stands at the ready to secure for you the hope of Him for all time. The way of God is favoring and true. None is better or with the knowing way of feeding the heart. God is the option of gold to the spirit. In God is the ability to maintain all of man's decision making; yet, He has a justified way in where He accepts man's initiative as his own. If a person is unwilling to follow the love of God to the grave, he has that stand and God won't interfere. However, the path to death is a negative and God would rather all of mankind be a witness for the good way. God has not torn away the veil to cause harm or a negative. He made the way for man to know Him in a personal manner by offering the Blood of Jesus so man could gain in the just way of hope. It may seem unreal but serve the Lord and you will achieve the life of good known character. It will represent the Lord and it will garner to man the truth of Christ to his spirit. Leading so others find the unity is wise and good and we need to invest in it thoroughly.

God is care to the heart none other has the ability to offer. In His way is the witness of trust necessary to bring into play the love of Him. All of mankind is who God witnesses toward. The one who believes is given salvation and in this act is life eternal. The glory of God is not a simple gesture but rather one of hope and guiding. Many believe to follow God means little reward when in truth it is the way for life to be a blessed time frame. The Word of the Living God is far superior to that of any read of its kind for there is no better witness than Scripture. The light of the trust one gains is solid and with support leading to a better enhancement of Jesus. The bounty is far reaching and many gain in the way of support. God aligns the heart with the initiative of Him so better thought processes build. The glory of Christ is far reaching so know when you share His truth others learn and are rewarded. Even this tiny stand I have of giving someone attention carries with it the hope of God. For this I am eternally grateful. I will never walk without the saving power of God for there is no other way more beneficial to me than God's favor. Knowing the reward guarantees me the hope of a lead in the way of fruit that lasts for all time. I have captured the willing with love and shown them how to find faith. This to me is the stand of life I bear witness to.

The knit value of the One who made me is what I strive to represent. In Him I have the gift of love needed to carry others to Him. God leads with character, and He never forgets my heart in the process. The unity is a sight I lean forth to. The ability to give another the love of the great I Am is a plan I intend to pursue. Walking in the favor of light is a reward where I am made righteous. There resides the unity but still I am my own person. I can attribute my hope to Christ and in doing this attaining the bounty from Him that is complete. I have the knowing aptitude of calling others by way of my demeanor. It is not difficult to offer love to another and it encapsulates me with character toward him. I value mankind in where I now retrieve the heart a stand of love and unity. It comes to me due to my effort applied to His way. The great One of all is my beloved. I reach for His value, and I gain the way of trust. He is the maintenance of a mighty goal, and I am blessed by Him. To unify with Him is a value many have understood. It is real and genuine and in Him is the sight needed to flourish. Only the Living Word stands as right for God is this gift.

1 In the beginning was the Word, and the Word was with God, and the Word was God. John 1:1 NIV

My net worth has risen far above my own understanding. I have not cash to feed my heart for it is taken away and placed in another's grasp. But the value of my inheritance far surpasses this gain. I have the knowing ability to abide in the care and the honor of the Risen I Am. I am leading in where my heart knows my work efforts mean another learns and is fed hope. To deliver the path to any in need gives me the hope I am making a difference for Christ. I know He is not in need of my work efforts but to Him it shows my support in such a way that there is no denying He is my hope and gain. I have the knowing of a child in the early stage of learning for I did not apply my life to spiritual leading from the Lord. It took the faith of trust for it to blossom and develop forth for goodness. I now realize had I intended to make a stand for God early in my growing I would be safe with Him at this time. But I must be a witness today due to my unity to the Savior. He has made me an honorary spokesperson on His behalf, and it pleases me to do so. The love of the One who masters the drive and cultivates it into love is a committed Being of justification. I learn and teach where the door opens and that is what staples me to the knowledge others need God too. I have the hope of leading mankind into the area of salvation, and I know Jesus is the gift of that topic. In Him is the unity no other can perform or establish. The role of meeting man to invest for his livelihood is new and endearing all at the same time. God has perfect unity, and He knew how best to describe the way forward. It was a unity I knew I could delve forward to. I wake up and the first prayer is for another to gain the knowledge I now possess. The topic of conversation in the break room is never light filled or holy but rather that of nonsense and sexuality. The speech causes my stomach to churn, and I lose the value to many. If God shows me someone not willing to act in such a manner, I know he is either one of God's or he is thinking to be for the light is still within him. The beauty of the witness provides me with a goal of sharing how to offer the knowing ability and to give the love I have to him with full presence in the light. God is the goal, not my own manner. The real value is the King and I worship Him with freedom in the quiet. My love burns within, and I stand in the wake of His glory fed with truth and honor.

God is not the one who made me to stand against His wise knowledge. It was my own less than understanding and all I desired was to know how to have a good time and influence others to do the same. To party meant to have a witness of friends and monetary goods. I never wondered what more there was to life itself. I have the realization I knew little about growing in care or support. But today I have the reasoning of a mature person who knows the heart and the unity of the Most High. I entertain where He alone is the one I shower my mind to. I have the will to have family or friends in my home but today that is considered not to be favoring to the community. We are forbidden to engage in offerings of love in that manner. Even the less than perception of no unity is thought of as having value. How deceived the people have become! The ones who do not follow the path of the sovereign God of mankind have no hope nor will they. To know the work of the Lord and to offer it forward assures me I am more than a message of little knowledge but rather that of fruit bearing for the spirit. I have the will to stand in courage and to unite with the people who follow my way of thinking, but we aren't permitted to speak in a cordial manner. If we are overheard, we are sent to a facility where we are trained to hate and gift no love. It is supposed to represent freedom but to me it is all death contained in the form of no beauty. God is a bright love, and He supports the man who harvests the heart toward His person. The great way to feed others is to invite them into your circle and to author for them the gift of a plan in where their hearts receive the light from on high. It travels from the forefront of the offering and leads to the plan of salvation. Where is the unity if not for mankind to know the Creator? He is the value of a bright will and trust. To know the One who made all of man is sight of birth leading to the clear view of wise unity. Does it mean you won't ever make a mistake? Hardly! No human is perfect. Only Jesus in man form walked with no sin. He was the one all could learn from; yet, men determined to crucify Him due to the evil within their hearts and minds. Many understood God was not the one who carried darkness but even that wasn't reason enough for him to offer up the unity. Man, alone, is without the knowledge of the faith. Only in Christ is man given the knowledge of character leading to unity and good harmony. How do I know this is true? No other has been as giving to me as Jesus has been. His life for mine was the stand He took, and I know I am more precious to Him than all the gold in the universe.

    Gain has the performance of providing the unity but without the support from Christ there is no hope. God can build and divide so He is able to maintain a good support measure at all times. In the way of faith God has the knowledge He is ever faithful to mankind. In Him is the witness all need to be intertwined with unity to Him. He made the earth and the animals, so He has no issue with you or me. He operates in character, and He never deviates from this goodness. The nearness of Him is where you invite Him to your person. The simplest outreach matters to Him, so believe you entertain Him when you look to Him with hope. The love of the care He provides is all fulfilled. You never have to wonder where your unity will materialize. It is always there within the heart if salvation has taken root. How does a person believe if he can't have the faith required to gain this guiding? Advance your heart by taking time to witness the love of Christ and acknowledge He is the one of hope. Ask and you shall receive is what the note taking reveals when Scripture is understood.

7 "Ask and it will be given to you; seek and you will find; knock and the door will be opened to you. 8 For everyone who asks receives; he who seeks finds, and to him who knocks, the door will be opened. Matthew 7:7-8 NIV

The character of the Living Word known as Christ is the knowledge we require to hold fast in times of trials and loss. The hope within man is able to bend and not break when the heart endures heartbreak. Many do not have this gift and they lay themselves at the altar of deceptive values. The people who care about value have silenced speech but are able to pray and be heard just the same. God is all things right and good, so I know He is able to justify my caregiving and put it forward to someone who needs aid. Were I to simply stop acting on behalf of God I would lose my witness and be of little support. I do not choose to step out of the ring of fire, but I shall be discrete and watch for God to acknowledge to me where to send a message of light. He cares for me and I in turn value His authority. We are tied spiritually and, in this gain, I have been kept safe. I know the time may come where I must stand in front of a firing squad, but I pray for courage to witness till the end. My testimony has value and even though I don't know who I have been informative toward I believe God works in my favor. To accept the love and care provided from above shelters me from the loss of no other's company. I do not invite affection, as it is not true favor but physical outreach and not value bearing. Where should I stand when the people before me come against the light? Should I accept defeat and say the truth, or should I remain discrete until God speaks and declares I am ready to divulge His way out loud? I have not understood I am to do this at this time, so I stay quiet and stand in the distance when another condemns my Savior. I do not rejoice publicly for fear of losing my own hope to be alive. God will offer the directive and I shall hold fast to His counsel. In leading another one must accept there is a proper time and unity to say the light of God to others. God is the Master of all things good and true, so I know I am safe in His loving arms. He will not stand against me, and I shall bear witness to Him when He ordains it for me to do so. We are tied and I am standing on His way of being. I shall not lose my life until He plans for it to happen.

God is the one who made me, and in this unity I am found favoring. The love of Christ comes forward and I have the ability to garner to another the offered way. To align with the character of God is to offer to Him the necessary unity of hope. God supports my love and in Him is the character needed to gift many the pleasure of hope. I know I am not all-knowing, but I realize I am finding the truth to be productive to my heart. The unity is a factor I do not forget. Ever before my heart is the knowledge I am not alone in this hardened time frame. I love the way of faith and in it is the real meaning for mankind to find it abundantly. I never knew I could find happiness with the God of all but now I am in His will, and I have the hope of Him within me. He never loses my influence, but I offer to others the care of Him for the better of their well-being. The all-knowing God of mankind does not fail nor does He misstep or fail to guide. In the Word is the support I know I need to accomplish His goal making. The fact I have no authority to act does not mean I am without the unity of the saving power. I stand with the unity I have, and I know I am fed by the witness of Christ, and it offers me the value of a committed being who never fails. I have the hope of God due to reading the many verses He has provided my heart. How do I know it is a gift of faith? I never feel alarmed or without hope when I receive the care gift. To know the light is from God is a value I have supporting my own manner. The trust of knowing my Savior is far better than any other insight or gift of support for God alone is the one I cleave to. He has prospered me when I lost hope and security. He supplied me with the courage to offer Him to another and in doing this act I gained the witness of knowing God is within me. I knew I could share Him, and the courage came to me due to the belief I am in His honor. To know the One who made all things good is to understand God is complete and holy.

The way of study is solid, and I now have many items of wealth. I have prayer and the knowledge of Scripture, so I am prepared to offer another the benefit of faith. I write when I am able, but I know one may find my offered light and turn me over to the authorities. I know this may happen, but until then I will apply to memorization and gain in this way. My heart fills with courage where I focus my love to Him, the great One of trust. I know I have the knowledge of mankind as well as that of the One who crafted me. Knowing the lighted path far exceeds the loss of knowledge from mankind. It is far better to operate with character and live in health than to offer no communion to man. I have never been one to stand on the sidelines but now I am forced to record in the quiet where another is sending light my way. I can't simply profess the hope I own but rather I need to act quietly with care from on high. God is the way to thrive and in Him I will reside. The gift of knowing this secures my resource of value and I favor my God with hope. He has made for me the path of trust and in doing so I now remain committed to many in need. I pray throughout the day and I act according to the way of God, but I do not present as such. I formulate a path, and in the knowledge, I have a witness of standing. To ponder where I will end is not for me to do as God supports me at this time. I will never fade from His offered goal, so I know the value of me is extensive. The unity I have is far-reaching and in the course of knowing my God I have favor leading to unity. None can compare in this way. God the Father is a caregiver and in His manner is light for all those who choose to gain. Any who wish to find the faith need only to invite Him within. It seems too easy and I for one used to believe such foolishness. Today I am in the knowing group of the ones who determined God was good and right. Due to this unity, I have the trust and care I dreamed of. All the manner of the light is for the measure of faith to thrive. I know I have the trust of God as He has made me in His image, and I have chosen Him as my partner.

The face of a person bears witness to the known power of the path of trust when God is the one, he believes in. The all-knowing Savior is righteous and true. God leads in the way of faith so support the work you offer and prepare for gain to come. God is perfect and righteous. He does not fade into the dark for there is no darkness within Him. He is perfect with purpose for mankind. I benefit with hope when I support Him and in doing this act righteousness unfolds. To align my spirit with the moral code of God is to stand with character and witness the growth of Him within me. The unity gains me recognition, and in this way, I find the trust to proceed even when it is hard to do so. The value of living in this era of time is the remembering of how things were before the disappearance of the people who had belief in Christ. It happened before I was ready so today, I stand in the loss. But I have the knowledge God is all-knowing and in Him is the knowledge I need for support to be real. I work for the better of my team, but it is hard as many only dream of more wealth of the pocketbook. I have understood this is the draw for many of mankind. I now know I used to act in the same way. Today I reveal I was lost and without hope due to not uniting in character to the loving King. I had the option, but I felt I could do better without the love of Him. My understanding was weak, and I lost the goal my grandmother placed for me to gain from. Due to her administering to me I was given the hope and now I believe. This knowledge floods my heart and mind. To know God cares even when I don't accept Him showers me with value. Today, I hope to be an instructive partner to others. I had my own agenda and I felt I could make decisions that would prosper me. How little I gained I dare not even contemplate for my outlook was so dire and uninformed. With hope I have the ability to stand in the way of favor leading to the value of support necessary for others to learn and harvest reliance from on high. God is the support beam I know is good and harmonizing within me. Today, I have the commitment of faith and in the knowing I share where able.

5

Glory is Rising in My Heart

I have the knowing sound judgment that there is unity in the way I operate. I came to the Lord in a free manner and in doing so I now have the worship time necessary to thrive. Due to my time of prayer, I believe I gain in the way of true faith. The Lord sustains my every goal and makes me a living sacrifice to many. I stand in this hope, and I now have the gift of salvation which ties me to the One of great truth. With character I have the hope of future leading and in the way of favor I support the ones who lead me in their direct line of sight. A simple gesture comes forward, and then I maintain the heart with a smile and a nod. It's simple; yet, so meaningful in this time of heartbreak. Little transpires where others are fed due to those who watch and hope to eliminate the prosperity of love. No one believes we are at an end to the way of faith for God is better than the death man has incorporated. Man will lose the battle and favor will come into play. Jesus will garner Himself to the land of His heritage at the Mount of Olives East of Jerusalem. I know this due to the verse of stand I was given. It supports this knowledge and I engage with the reasoning of it.

4 On that day his feet will stand on the Mount of Olives, east of Jerusalem, and the Mount of Olives will be split in two from east to west, forming a great valley, with half of the mountain moving north and half moving south. Zechariah 14:4 NIV

God is formidable and holy to the core of Him. With character God has gifted mankind the will of His heart. If study is applied, you will find the unity and a manner of stand will develop. God is all-knowing and He hears how you portray His operating manner. If you believe; yet, walk outside Him there is no faith within you. Man is weak and at times he makes poor decisions but when God is the focal point love abounds. To stray and leave God then return means the angels above rejoice. God has never left someone in need, however, if you choose to stay in a life of sin where is the love to Christ? Knowing He is all things right and true means man is not without hope. The love and care of God is sharing in the way of true honor and favor toward another individual. If all you dream of is sharing the witness of faith, God has you as His counterpart. The reading of the Word places the heart in the hand of Jesus and in the manner of faith great unity is projected. God is all things righteous and holy. He cannot sin. He is Scripture and in Him is the unity of love and insight. To have the stand of knowing where to operate is a gift in the way of faith. God supports the one who determines He is the better way.

10 In the same way, I tell you, there is rejoicing in the presence of the angels of God over one sinner who repents." Luke 15:10 NIV

God is the way to prosperity. To trust Him with your heart and mind is to believe He will advance your spirit toward His heart. God is true to His Word. He never disagrees with His Bible. I have many who deem me not of good harmony due to the way I interact with them. I do not evaluate them as good and in this knowledge, I separate my work from theirs. Should this mean I lose my life I must stand in the way of unity to the Living God I call Savior. He is more precious to me than any work plan. I know simple work is easy and I offer more than this to appease my manager but in doing so I draw more interest than I like. How shall I offer the insight I have without losing my own stand of life? God is my main concern so I shall invest where the door is open. How this happens will be from God alone and not my own ideas. I have the realization to wait for Him to perform on my behalf. At times this is difficult, but I know the value is there. I shoulder the burden of no offered goal and in this knowledge is the witness I am not without scrutiny. I have the ability to push harder, but then I would not gain a single moment of my own. People who have given their work the manner of all their heart have died in the ambush of no leisure. The ability to savor time has been banned so now we must work into the night as well. I have no doubt this will include longer hours and more hard labor if one does not comply. Gone is the reason to venture into management. There is no bounty there just death and no hope. I have seen the management team fade into the black line of no life, and it happens rapidly. The witness is one of scare tactics and we lose our pension if we don't move up the food chain. I have been sloppy on purpose so as not to perform in such a way I can't continue to meet new members here at this dark facility. I have the knowledge time is becoming an entity that only the wealthy can obtain. I know it is not the way of God, so I plan on marketing a path to stay out of the limelight. I believe the expectation of me has dropped; and for this I am grateful. I will, however, value the work for it maintains my role of a witness for Christ.

The love of Christ is for all of man to find unity when he offers his heart to the Creator. This is a gesture of faith and in it is the reward of justified gain. Where God is granting knowledge fruit is found. If the storm of life has held you for a time you know it takes stamina and insight to offer others any line of feed that supports them. Where the heart is fed true knowledge is in play. God is the one who developed the knowing way to offer another the goal of Him. Have you been fed from another's hand? Did you gain or were you alone in the quest of hope? If you value the unity of God, you will garner forward the favor and you will inherit the witness of true love. God is the way to have favor. In Him is the trust and will to carry another to the heart of Him. God supports the many who have belief and who entertain Him without an expectation of goods returning to him. God is a provider of sight not just money and grandstanding. God is the Waymaker of the heart. He establishes the heart, and it is gifted true favor in where the bounty is seen as right not just a gift of leading. In the way of knowing the one who favors your heart, comes the beauty of a stand of leverage that meets the spirit in the way of trust to leading. God captures the heart, but He does not override it. In the commitment is the insight of a stand of good character. The way to align with good value is to adjust the heart in the area of favor not reflection of any heart value. The kindred person seeks to learn and prosper in faith, and he applies his heart to the Scriptures of the Word. The value of God is far better than money in the account at the bank. In God is the value of life eternal and it shines in a bright manner. The way to offer this to others is to plan to emit a solid goal of faith. And act in the way of committed leading that justifies the unity and favors the union of God to man. I have the value of the Risen Savior and I offer it where able. In today's market it is difficult, and I must wait upon an open door to do so. At one point there will come a loss to me due to someone learning my unity to God for it is forbidden to discuss. I have shared many times the fruit of a smile and yet none have burdened me for it. This I know is a card of hope from on high. God leads me to the one who is searching and in need. I have the mustard seed quality and I set my heart toward the many that require support. Prayer is the gift I can provide with no one realizing it is taking place. God is all-knowing so I pray in a silent manner and induce the covering of a good, committed plan. I have the way of faith and in the conquest of a prayer many are found favoring the way of God. The unity is received, and holy meaning is portrayed.

There is support to any who proceed in favor and who offer their hearts and minds in the direct line of action leading to others having the will of God to their hearts. Many have the aptitude to secure a plan in motion; yet, they feel lost as to how to proceed. Prayer brings forth the knowing way to align and offer insight. It takes the heart time to believe in the power of the Mighty King so invest and wait with expectation. God will not fail you in the dream. The one who accepts the goal will procure a unity and there will reside a step in motion garnering a way ahead. God is the one to gift the trust and in Him is the ability to stand in a secure way. He invests where He is welcomed so act with honor and invite the King into your person. He will be an invested partner who offers you growing aptitude in where many have the same outreach and mission. Working with others is a goal to give hope in. I lead where I can but today this is in the quiet whereas years prior, one could speak in an outward way. If I had but determined the better path, I could have spoken in favor of God and led many more to the life-giving hope of Jesus. I have settled the thought process and I do not dwell upon what might have been. I know the value of where I am and how I am serving others with character. This is a dark period in history, but light does shine. If one searches, it can be had. Love is not abundant so I know what little I can offer is received when hope is sought. I have the witness of a good employee, but I do not apply too much as to stay concealed within my own corner of the department. Working leads to recognition and I do not wish to have this happen. To lead with a quiet manner is how I operate and compel others to guide in their market. Leading is a gift and I value the option of it. If I find I am in danger, I simply walk to the end of the room and discontinue the act of a witness. Confusion sets in so none have truly heard me confess the goal of salvation. I know I have the way of God so I act as though I am dumbfounded in where none can comprehend where I stand. But if there is an open doorway to lead, I continue to offer light. If it is received and trust in hope builds, I know I can express more than just a quick glance. Together with favor I have accumulated a following of faith-built people who themselves are actively trying to share the Gospel. It is something we discreetly offer one to another by way of eye contact. Reassuring ourselves we are tied with virtue. The goal is to gift others the lead of salvation so they too can administer to another in freedom. We have the unity and in our way of being sheltered we grant hope to those who look for a witness of light. It is gratifying to know I am not the only one operating in the danger Zone. I would not wish this lifestyle on another, but it is the day and time we find ourselves in. I accept this is life, but I am not defeated to it. God is conquering my doubt and building me forward for His glory.

To evolve with character and entertain the spirit of light is a support beam of unity in where love is offered freely. God does not tally our sins against us. He puts in motion a pathway where we are fed with unity and our digestive tract is all within. He feeds our hearts and minds with value, and we connect to Him with trust. Our desire is to stand in the way of a goal that builds with volume in where hope and beauty are combined. God leads the man willing to aspire to the region of a stand He has ordained. I know the way to connect with God is reading the fruit of His Word. I have documented many verses for others to gain as well. It has been inspiring to report the truth to the ones seeking to know God. I have the knowledge I am a caregiver and I represent light to many. I realize I am not the one to carry the heart, but I am sufficient enough to divulge the truth of God. He has enlightened me in the way of support and in this unity; I comprehend who He is as a God of hope and enduring light. The all-knowing plan of God is for me to light the way for many to find Him. I have the faith I will lead others to Christ, and I am secure in this unity. I know I am without a stand if I fade out of favor, and I have no intention of doing such a foolish thing. God is the real favor of hope. He is the gift all mankind is in need of. I can't imagine where I would be now had I not accepted the unity God offered. I would be alone in my longing and there would be no reason for me to continue working. For even though we gain in the cash department we are not given the right to spend freely. No offering comes and we operate with no guiding. God is the One I serve while I implement the goal of faith. Due to the One who mastered the craft I gain with insight. The love and care of Jesus is all complete. It is me who is not fully developed.

The unity of the One who made you is that of a right bearing and holy giving. God, the one who developed the way to plan, is the same influence of a stand of support none can compare to. God is glory to the heart and in Him is the unity of trust requiring a goal of developed favor. How does He operate when no faith is put forth? Only He, Himself, can answer that question but I do believe He knows when there is a sliver of insight, and He offers it forward to benefit the manner of intake to claim Him. I know He is wise and in Him is the redeeming way of favor for all who place their hearts and minds in His care. The One of hope bears witness to our hearts and in the process, favor is bestowed. I have the value system of a pure will in need of the One who made her. I have the aspect of truth because He gave me the understanding. The way of knowing who the operative is and who is the claimed is made known by the character of the Risen God. I have the knowledge God operates with support due to the acknowledgement He has given me favor even when I don't deserve it. In the plan for man to prosper comes the alignment He is the sight birth of true witness making. I have the full percentage of a gift of unity on the back of faith. In the making of this tie, I am standing in faith due to the unity of God to me in a personal way. He presses forward my love and care and in the act of giving I gain Him for my own stand. I have seen many who believe I am without knowledge due to the fact I portray I am not holding a degree of education beyond that of a high school diploma. I have, however, the factoring of a person who is capable of giving others knowledge that lasts through eternity. The plan of salvation is far better than the education of man. In the making of a righteous way, I know and envision a unity none other can compare with. I understand God alone is the one who maintains my heart. I have the value of this in my heart thanks to the plan my God provided at Calvary where He hung in pain and bled for my security to be eternal. I now prepare for many to learn this support. I have the complete unity necessary to receive a lighted path to God. In the way of faith, He delivers this with honor. I thank Him with respect and love for He is the trust machine I bear witness to.

My care has a price tag of hope. I am the favor of light known as a bride member. God has supported me with this knowledge, and I learn due to the way He invests in me. I am a knowing sidebar of growth due to His manner not that of myself. I love to hear His counsel and to see Him with clear vision. This comes when I act as a person in love with her Savior by applying my heart and stand toward Him.

The value of knowing the great One of faith is more than I can compare for there is none more trustworthy than Christ. He has me in complete unity to His way and I engage in a free way due to His call to me. In knowing He does not fail me nor will He, I have comfort. Love is a unity I admire and holdfast to. God is the one who made me care about those in need. It came by way of a light to my heart. I did not stand in this truth until I invited Him into my mind with trust. The invitation was a sight plan of faith I believed would make a difference in me. I gained life eternal and in the making of salvation I was gifted unity. How can there be something so good; yet, so many don't believe? I was one of those people. I never thought I would aspire to entertain the One who made all mankind. I simply set my heart and mind into the idea of a future with only myself as the administrator of my heart. I was in darkness and loss was building. I didn't think so at the time but now the vision speaks this truth. To allow the One who made heaven and earth to work within me has been a dream of favor supportive to my heart. I learn and prosper in where all my heart learns and gains. God is the one I gravitate to as He supports me so well. I am not alone, nor will I ever be since the acceptance of Jesus to my person. I value this relationship and it grants me the role of truth to my heart. I offer the love of Christ to those in need and all my yearning is for He who is the great Waymaker.

I have no greater offering, and I acknowledge there never will be. I have gained the mind of a child in where I have the faith like one in innocence. The love of God carries with it the ability to obtain the light and to spread it to many. Days of pondering what to think upon have faded for God is the one I learn by. I invest in reading Scripture He has bestowed to my heart. I record what I gain so another can read and learn too. It is a gift I have been given and I shall not regret it for its value can't be measured or contained. How do I hear from the God of all? It comes in a small voice of understanding with clear intent that is right and true. I have the hope others will learn this as well, so I stand in prayer and unity. The role of me to those I see is to offer them trust when there is little to share. I give the heart a nod and the smile of hope to invite them forward in care. Light abounds if someone is trying to find it. This is a strange time to be residing in, but I know there is a purpose to it. I shall inquire to Christ and wait for a response knowing He has more understanding than I.

10 I delight greatly in the LORD; my soul rejoices in my God. For he has clothed me with garments of salvation and arrayed me in a robe of righteousness, as a bridegroom adorns his head like a priest, and as a bride adorns herself with her jewels. Isaiah 61:10 NIV

5 As a young man marries a maiden, so will your sons marry you; as a bridegroom rejoices over his bride, so will your God rejoice over you. Isaiah 62:5 NIV

God speaks to the one who is willing to hear. In His way of being man finds the unity needed to push ahead and move with character. God is all care and no doubt. He offers the heart the way to proceed, and the way of His being is light at all times. This is the right path to follow. I stand with the trust of Him within me due to Him saving my heart as His own. Yes, I fail at times; yet, I am made complete in His favor. The unity of me to Him is a gift I shall never reject. It is too good not to savor for all time! Time is fading into a black abyss and all the many who have determined they would take the mark are losing their souls to Satan. He is the one who has placed the hardship upon those who reject his way of being. Even the ones who have chosen his way are leading lives of devastation. He is not the way to find eternal peace. He only implants lies and no gain. How am I withstanding the pressure not to unite to his character? I do not listen to his speeches, nor do I engage on televised outreach. I know his way is to claim any who are not walking in truth, and I know deception is rampant. I look to the counsel of

Scripture for the right way to operate. It alone is the vested way to align the heart toward hope. God is more than an idea, so I stand with His manner not the enemy's. God is the way to find prosperity and in Him is the path of leading that puts in motion the way to live in a justified pathway. I love my King and Savior and I shall always entertain Him within me. He has laid claim to me in a gesture of unity, and we are tied for all time. This is perfect and good, and I shall not want for God is the light to me and I embrace it.

I am here as a provider of hope to the many who have come before me with an outreach in eye contact. But this is not to say I have known all who were pretending. God is the one who stood on my behalf and guided me into the knowledge of the faith bearing. The blankness of a non-believer is made to be expressed but if there is a person searching, I have been given the insight so I work in character to this opportunity. I miss at times and questions come my way, but I have avoided the direct term of a witness simply by remaining in the quiet without answering in the way they expect. I do not deny my Lord and Savior, but I do not express who is His if someone is suspect to hate. For there will only be a managed fight that ensues. But where man has asked direct leads, I offer the truth of what I have learned. These are the ones looking for the goal of receiving the light and the knowledge then is placed in a subtle contact. I may leave a note card or a prayer for them to read in where I offer the presence of God to them. I have never been convicted but I know it could happen. If the wrong individual assumes I am aiding in the faith of God I will be prosecuted and hung in the town square. But for now, I work as a unity maker, and I cooperate to the will of the team I work with. I will not take on a workload that leaves me staggering but I do act as a member who has a vested care. I know many follow my lead and work as I have been so this means the goal of God is progressing. I have acted according to the way of Jesus. And I have the gift of sharing Him even though I may not have the reward of knowing how I have reached another I believe it is there nonetheless. The ability to offer others the way I have chosen is a will to favor them with true love and a secure desire of faith. God is the one doing the heavy lifting. I merely am the connection of relay.

God supports the many that are tied to Him in the best way possible. It is the wealth of the need that one makes the enduring hope thrive. It is God above who harvests the will and who offers it forward. I know I have the ability to take many toward the love of Jesus, but will there be time enough? I have not the inherent growing ability leading to others where I work. There are only a few who come my way, however, I know we tie together, and we operate with character in where more can learn from our endeavors. The witness of truth is all together that of a knowing God who has the witness through those who believe and have the value of Him as their counterpart. God cares for all mankind and in Him is the love of a sound gain. God is the unique being who maintains our knowledge and makes it thrive. I have the faith due to the One who made me a person of value and support. I lead in the same way as the saving One for He is the guide I believe in.

I can be a simple piece of light, but I do offer the unity it claims. Light of the heart is the missile that rewards the heart and mind. They have meaning. When the knowledge of the Waymaker is prospering leading comes into play. The heart yearns to lead due to the hope of sharing the light and its desire of true gain is heard. The value of the Waymaker cannot be understood but the work of Him is witnessed by way of favor to the many who inquire as to where to learn of the Savior. God supports the person who is asking and who knows the truth is something to learn and invest in. Rejection sets the lie in cement and the more it is embraced the farther into the darkness one travels. At one point there is never going to be acceptance due to the hardening of the Spirit. Believe in the One with the fist invitation and you will be garnered with redemption. The value of knowing the Almighty far surpasses that of any officer of the law or famed leader. Man is weak without the protective layer of Jesus. He is not able to bear witness to anything good without Him. Souls are not forsaken. They stand in doubt and refuse to claim the Lord of good hope; in doing so no eternal guidance can be had. Devastation is what rewards the one who doesn't invite Jesus within. It is the way of life, and all must choose the path they will be fed from. Glory is Jesus and a true need is made vital by way of knowing the truth from the curse of Satan. The unity of Christ is a gain in where true knowing comes forth. The love administered from on high is equal to that of none other than God for there is no better way.

I have the knowing part of salvation so I can offer it forward and it is within my heart I do so. I am one to align with unity, so another finds the faith as I have. Why do I try when I could lose my life? It is far too important for others to gain salvation than it is for me to fear for my own freedom. Either way it is gain for I will spend eternity with the great One of hope. If I die and if I stand for a time I will have an investment in where others find prosperity in the Savior, too.

21 For to me, to live is Christ and to die is gain. Philippians 2:21 NIV

God is the one who develops forth work of Him to another waiting to gain in His way. The offered way is from on high and all of mankind is the reason for the outreach.

God is not the one who stands at a distance for He loves all who profess Him as faithful. He is the one smitten with the people He has known. We are born into the light when we embrace the Creator and the call from Him. It happens when we can relate to Him in a personal way. Even a little child can learn who God is and why he needs to have a secure relationship to Him. We forget children are bounty to Christ just as they are to the ones who fostered them in the way of parenthood. The manner of favor from God far exceeds what man is capable of providing. Even though at times there is doubt about the One who gifts truth it can't negate He reaches those in need. The love of the One who made you never ceases to work within your scope of understanding. Where the faith is centered, the unity is adhered to. God is the way to prosper and in Him is the reason to stand in awe of His mastering. I know I am not one to have the whole unity without the love of the One who created my heart. He knew from the start how to offer me the Word and when I would accept His invitation of hope. With the nourishment of Him to my soul I stood with character and tied my heart to Him in a personal way. It stands as a witness I am one in Him. He has been my lead through this difficult era. If I had not desired Him and accepted His call, where would I be today but in the dark with no insight leading no one to a better way? I know I need my Savior above all things, and I am glad to offer Him to any in my region. I have the will to announce this, but it is not the time as God has not instilled this to my spirit. But when the time comes to stand before God, I will have a confession of faith in where I will be safe from harm due to the realization and acceptance of the Savior to me. I know and stand on the promise I am saved, and I have the spirit of Him delivered to me personally. I do not lose in this administering for God is the one of beauty and it is Him that feeds my heart. I value my God above all, and I am committed to Him for the duration. We are a team of a stand in where no other will ever break our unity.

God expresses His role of faith to the one who believes and invites His character. He is not the one to push His way forth. If you reject Him, you are the one taking your own self out of the equation. There will be no light for you and darkness will continue to grow in your spirit. You won't understand what it is that is taking form but know others will see the darkness. If you value the unity and the spiritual connection to a bright Being of hope rely on the Savior for there is only one God. The spiritual connection will be the reason for you to stay committed and in doing this action you will partner with the One of true gain. I can't begin to state enough God is the one who made all things right and good and in death without Him you will only witness darkness and no guiding information will reside. A loss will be what holds you fast and there will be no escape.

I am a Scared Witness

Man is not equipped to survive the death experience but once; yet, in hell that is all one will know. How is this fair? The rejection of Mighty God is to declare you do not wish to have Him present within you or in your daily life. So He accepts this rejection and places you where He is not at. It is an understanding few realize or are willing to entertain. If people knew from others what death held, they would investigate it with open hearts. But many are unwilling to tame the deceptiveness of Satan and let him work within without knowing what true light represents. Hell is not a place of beauty, as God the Creator is the light bulb to man. Without the character of God there is no hope only darkness and despair.

22 "The time came when the beggar died and the angels carried him to Abraham's side. The rich man also died and was buried. 23 In hell, where he was in torment, he looked up and saw Abraham far away, with Lazarus by his side. 24 So he called to him, 'Father Abraham, have pity on me and send Lazarus to dip the tip of his finger in water and cool my tongue, because I am in agony in this fire.' 25 "But Abraham replied, 'Son, remember that in your lifetime you received your good things, while Lazarus received bad things, but now he is comforted here and you are in agony. 26 And besides all this, between you and us a great chasm has been fixed, so those who want to go from here to you cannot, nor can anyone cross over from there to us.' 27" He answered, 'Then I beg you, father, send Lazarus to my father's house, for I have five brothers. Let him warn them, so they will not also come to this place of torment.' 29 "Abraham replied, 'They have Moses and the Prophets; let them listen to them.' 30 "No, father Abraham,' he said, but if someone from the dead goes to them, they will repent.' 31 "He said to him, 'If they do not listen to Moses and the Prophets, they will not be convinced even if someone rises from the dead.'" Luke 16:22-31 NIV

When I offer another the knowledge I have learned it stands in support of the Living Word. God, my Caretaker is all right and surefooted. He values me far more than I can imagine. Due to His saving witness, I am made whole. He is the light I contain and in Him is the fruit of a spiritual goodness. He speaks with character and in Him is bounty I care to embrace. I receive a good mental unity and I thrive due to Him. With the bond of knowing Him comes the reward of being in His care. The support of His hold is built upon the knowledge of His goodness. I read and invite His Word to my heart and in doing this action God favors me. I know reading Scripture is the best way to find unity and I witness this daily. I have the yearning to be with Christ, but I know the time has not come. But when it does, I will be ready. How this happens only God knows the answer to. My expectation is to stand in courage and value His heart with the unity and the goal of Him to my person. God, the one who made me His, is the support measure I have needed to flourish. I have the aptitude to witness and in doing this act I find unity and courage. He is the one who maintains the heart, but it is through me that He operates. Does He need me to offer another His leading? No, for He is all gain. But He has chosen us, His Christ like people, to witness so others find the faith needed to be administered to. Why I am here for such a time as this only He has the answer to. But I am secure in the offering, and I gain in response to Him.

15 When they had finished eating, Jesus said to Simon Peter, "Simon son of John, do you truly love me more than these?" "Yes, Lord," he said, "you know that I love you." Jesus said, "Feed my lambs." 16 Again Jesus said, "Simon son of John, do you truly love me?" He answered, "Yes, Lord, you know that I love you." Jesus said, "Take care of my sheep." John 21:15-16 NIV

God is supporting the one who has His best interest in mind. God the Father and Jesus are one in the way of unity. They think as one and offer all their way of presence. In the power they hold many now know where to be standing. God is the way to a better heart intake in where truth is maintained. To pray and offer the love of Christ forward is to better your own perspective and find trust blossoming. I have the knowing ability to withstand the wind and its advancement but when the tide of loss comes forth, I believe I will withstand that too. God is the Waymaker and in Him I have the knowing way of manner supporting a team of employees. They do not share my courage, but they see me work with hope. This is unusual and they know there is something different within me. I know I am not without harm, if I intend to pursue this offering. But to be standing in the army of the Most High grants me the faith I can achieve in the way of a committed bond and goal. God is the light measure, and I am His offered lead. I do not entertain the role of no hope due to the will of Jesus within me. He is the guide I need to operate in a dismal world. I have the unity to align with His character and I know I am fed by His spiritual connection. The love of God is all entangled with power and it feeds the one who hears His voice. The reason I can go forward into the fire is I know God has me in the palm of His hand. I am standing with matrimony and a gain of value that incorporates the love of Him. I am dear to Him, and I know I will offer this same advantage to others in where the love I project will shine with hope. Today many have lost their knowledge and embraced the dark one who only seeks to ruin their testimony and steal their lives. I know better and I give this offering in a free manner. I love the goal seeking individual who believes there is another way to be. That is the person I inspire. God protects me in the unity and in Him I have the ordination of a true warrior on His behalf. I thank Him for the way He has claimed me. In doing so, I know the value of a ministry in where simple acknowledgement stands as righteous fruit. I am loved and I protect those who claim God. I offer them a viable partnering that is tied to Christ and His way.

My trust in the One who made all things beautiful is far greater than that of a man who offers no fruit. The value of the support measure can't be determined due to the vast way of operating in holy guiding. I know I am not the One to follow; yet, I turn my heart to the great way of Jesus, and I learn by His witness. The support I now show is for those who are looking to pursue the Risen Light and to align with Him for unity to be made just. God is the one I deliver my forward unity to. In Him is the ability to maintain my knowledge and guide it to a bloom stage of sight. I never wash my heart of this gift for it is the reward I receive with trust. I see many who never have the stand of favor for they have taken the mark of the Antichrist and now have no path to gain the light. The intent of God is for all mankind to invest in Him but not all do so with character. The many that distance their hearts from the Savior have only a distraction within them. Where the light resides, man has the unity to hear the voice of the Creator. In the offered way of Him hope is gained, and support resides. God is the gift to lead by. He is not a wayward loss nor is He one to align with sin. He is pure and in Him is the trust of all things good. I know the One who gave me insight stands with unity and in this offered way I turn to Him with my soul in line with His trust. How does this knowledge come to me? I work for the Lord by reading and applying my heart in His direction. This is due to the need of Him near to me. I do not walk in faithlessness, for God is the way of hope. I have learned God is all giving and in Him is the way to obtain unity. There is no other who can counsel me in such good harmony. I gain by reading the hope He has shown me in truth. I record the words and compose the light. It is not a new teaching but rather the verses of Scripture written in the Biblical era. I know it is a special reward to me I am to give in a free manner. I do not charge for this knowledge, and I am united in the understanding. To have been chosen to recite the message of trust is something I shall not cast aside. Many here now have unity to the One of hope. We have been given sight and all record the Word for many. We are not demanding others to wage this goal for it is all in the heart of the believer. God is supporting me and the many who have claimed Him in this time of hardship. We know it is not the same as it was before the people were brought up to heaven for this time is for the rejected who have learned how to value the Risen Lord. If no value came from the rapture no light was gifted. It is due to the heart where one spends eternity. It does not rest on the Waymaker for He is willing to bring to Him any who claim Him as King. You too, can have the Mighty Lord as your inheritance. Trust Him and believe while embracing the light. It is not difficult to become a member of the bride of Christ. But not to believe and to push Him away is the answer in and of itself. You aren't given an option on judgment day as the record will already have been written. Some think they can outwit God the Father and talk their way into heaven's gate. This is foolishness. Desperation makes man act in foolish ways and many now are without the Lord and never will know Him. The value was rejected, and the love of self, stood stronger. I am not the Risen God, but I know Him as my Lord. I shall forever be with Him in spirit.

The faith of one who has known God is clear to him and the resource of the Waymaker ties mankind to the spirit with trust. The goal becomes the way ahead and it consists of knowing the Lord in a profound manner. The lift of the one who turns to the Word stands in a superior way. I have the ability to recite many verses due to memorization and belief. I work with the goal of gaining the knowledge to be standing with character. I have the plan of sharing my knowledge and I dream of being included in the witness of light. At heaven's door I shall gain entry and I will not be pushed aside to loss. Jesus will embrace me with His heart, and I shall rest in unity to Him forever. Such a beautiful expectation and in the way of knowing it is real I gain unity. The love of the One who made me is far-reaching so I don't have to wonder does He know me wherever I may be? I have the answer within, and I rest with support. The trust of God is not a slim unity for it is built with true hope which the Father grants when I lean into Him. I stand with the knowing ability I will not be without my God. He is always my lead and my Guidance Counselor. I have the will to be part of the missionaries who have spread the Word to others. I am included with the work of saints before me. I believe I now know where to witness and who to lead in the unity of God. I have the leading gift due to the goal of gifting God to others. Anyone who desires to offer the knowledge of God will stand in this manner and have the doorway presented to him. It is with the faith of a mustard seed I advance in care. I grow with the will of God to me. In doing this I do not walk outside His instruction. I have the knowing goal to seek my God and in doing this act I stand on His behalf. The leadership of Him to me is a glorious trust I have gained. I shall work for my Caregiver knowing in doing so I am light to another.

God is true in His calling to the many who claim Him as Lord. The one who believes is the one tied to Him with character. Knowing the value of God comes to the believer and in it is the whole package of Him. We find ourselves constructed to read Scripture and to apply it forward. If you do not wish to engage in the Book of life, you are not committed to God with true unity. You may realize He is the Lord of man, but the unity is not adhered to. Why do I say this? I have been the one who acknowledged the Savior but did not cleave to Him with support. In doing this I had no aid when the time of loss ensued. I was gifted the lean of maintenance, so I never was lifted to heaven. I thank God I did not die before I was standing in the light. If I had, I would now reside in darkness for all time. Hell is real and no other stand is clear. I know what the meaning of knowing Christ represents. There are many who profess to know Him but have no knowledge of His character. The search must provide the factoring of unity for it to be adhered to. Yet, on a deathbed confession the value can be in play and the work of the Savior can bring the unity. But is it worth the risk to offer no intent and gamble on the fact you may not be committed as you think? I would never stave off the reading of Scripture for a fruit of loss now that I have learned the truth of knowing God. It is far more valuable than any other practice. I look at where I was, and I accept it was my own mistake and not that of Christ. The Bible is the gift for man to flourish and grow forth to. God knows the heart, and in Him is the unity to realize where true treasure resides. If you think some other investment has a hold over your thought process, you need to dispose of it quickly. I had focus of self, so I lost the benefit of an early time of preparedness. Today, I know better; and I do not advance in the way of something that draws me too quick to it. If daydreams come that are not wise divulge this and move away from the pull. The battle is relevant and in the way of trust God desires complete commitment. If you know you are weak in some area of life work for the call to claim it. God supports man and He offers the faith a way ahead. You may have to seek counsel to know what is genuine within and what hold you can't release. To limit yourself in the way of the draw does not mean it has no hold. It is contained but in the act of it you still visualize it before the love of the Creator.

Work is not for me at this time; however, I must still proceed and make ends meet. Even if it is for the governing body and not my own benefit. I have the goal and the reasoning to advance my heart in the way of faith toward God and that is the way I prefer to lead. I now have little to stand with due to many having been found bearing forward in the way of no insight. They have given themselves over to Satan and now they are dark with no love. I must reassure my heart by noting God is not the one who made them advance away but their own hearts and minds would not invite the truth. I now realize I have the gift of support needed to advance the love forward. I shall only speak to the one who has not taken the sign of the Antichrist for there is no point in trying to witness to them. They are lost with no hope of ever finding faith. I know many sought to learn but they gave up and lost all guiding influence. I do not obtain the unity on my own merit, but it is God who delivers it to me. To know the One of man is a born lean I shall always apply. I have the knowing sight of a true gain, so I act with unity and a holy manner. I believe I am with the many that stand on behalf of the mighty Caregiver known as the great I Am. The Word of Scripture is a truth I have knowledge in, and I invite it into my daily practice. Should I leave a plan of this in my home, or would it indicate to others if I did? I shall pray and read truth for better understanding.

My support is not perfect, nor will it be until I am residing in Christ's home in heaven. But to stand in courage means I have the unity supporting my knowledge of God. I value my Savior and I offer to Him the plan of faith knowing He works miracles within my heart. I love Him with abandonment and there is freedom within Him. I know weakness is part of mankind's way, but I invite Jesus to clear my heart of any loss I may be carrying. I know to indulge in some sin is not a way to thrive, so I offer my heart and mind to Christ. He will lead me with the unity needed to stand so I do not fail in His way. I know I have enough standing that my witness carries me to Him. I shall offer my favor to the many that have seen my actions, and I will invest with character. I am not the Being of hope for I am mere flesh and heart whereas God is a being of only goodness. What His makeup consists of is not for me to say. How I know Him is through the knowledge He is a caregiver and righteous. To know the One who made my mind is to believe He will stand on my behalf when I am in need. I shall remain faithful in where I will invest in the care and support of Him where I feel led. I am not the one who makes man right. That is Christ Himself. I have the knowledge of what is good and what is mere temptation. To expect my heart to always be just is a commitment no man can obtain. I will work on my shortcomings and gain in the unity of the Most High. Value to God is what I mean to have and in Him is the light of the Word. By investing in the way of unity I gain and learn. He shall confront my heart where needed and in doing so I will hear the path to lead from. The ability to labor will reside and in the mist of the knowledge I will adhere.

My light is from the reasoning of the true nature of my King. In the way of unity, I have the faith needed to tell another of the goal of Jesus without losing my own heritage.

To unite to the Creator is sound thinking and it reflects the heart of my own trust. The witness of Jesus feeds the spirit and in the ability of faith I know the necessary way to guide. I have the support of the One who made all things good and right and this comforts me. My goal making is for many to have the gain I have faith in. I look at where I work, and I know there is little I can offer to any in need, but I still do what I am able. God is the lead I have that offers to me the unity so I can claim Him with faith. I do not think I am without loss, but I know I have the way of God within, and it aligns my heart with clear knowledge. The beauty of the One who maintains my love is far greater than my own value. I am not the One who made all of mankind and the animals upon the earth. I have the way of knitting others to Him though. A simple gesture of favor and eyes and ears witness hope. It plants the way to gain and in the manner of faith light comes into play. I know the one who believes in my insight finds the way to God due to his own acceptance of Him. God is the value of all that is light so one never has to acknowledge no unity to Him. I have seen the support of God and I believe he is favoring to all who place their heart in His hands. The value of God's care is more than simple guiding as man does. It is far superior to a human's claim. I have the gift of knowing my Savior and in Him I find the way to operate with true love. The battle of no inherit gain makes a person feel unloved and without unity. This is the difference of where one is fed or where one only believes he is. Digesting the understanding money is not the blood of the heart can be a rude awakening. Many have fallen due to them believing to author only fruit of the bank account was the way to pursue light. In the devils' way is this unity. He gifts man wealth only to deceive him into thinking he has conquered the true way to thrive. Nothing is more damning than the rich who have no value to God. They have gained riches that have no meaning so they will burn up when the judgment comes before them. God operates with precise care leading to eternal fruit that sustains the life duration of eternity. How is this possible? God has created the heart and mind to flourish in where a spiritual lead is what maintains them. To know the One of hope is to understand wealth to Him is the manner in which you determine the price of His blood. You either confess He is the way to life in where the heart has embraced Him as Lord, or you reject it for another source of feeding. Would you like for your child to choose something over you as their benefactor in where the heart does not love? Should you have the option of saving a fellow member of the family would you choose it above the wealth of the world? This is the same way to think about Christ in relationship to your heart. If He is the one, you have support in above any other unity then you are committed to Him with favor for life. Riches can be tempting but they hold no value in comparison to life with the King. Evaluate the need of your eternal witness. Do you embrace death and hope in the Father as your mainstay or is there something on this earth you want to complete first? Unity in God means you would choose Him above anything, heaven related or not. To shower your heart in the way of faith is to stand with purpose to God so another hears the witness and receives the love value. Look to where you apply your mind and know this is what you dream of. If you think about the value of God, and He is the one you divest your spirit toward, you have found the unity and the match is solid.

The heart of the One who invested in mankind is for all to receive and benefit from. The favor is a gift and in it is the will of the Creator. How do I remain standing when no fruit is coming my way? It is due to the love of Christ and His lead in me. I know I am not the one to do the work or the noting, but I do offer a plan forward for any looking for insight. I have the gift of writing the verses to concrete pads, so others learn too and in doing this action others find the support they need to prosper. Many are now working in the same manner as God benefits all who call upon His name. I have the knowing gift of where to offer my knowledge due to God sharing this knowledge within me. I am not the way, but I do make the stand with harmony to His manner. The light I have supports the many that come and seek to learn more. They, too, are given support and other gifts of the heart are bestowed toward them. I have the knowing ability to offer the sight due to the One who made all as a body of faith. We act in accordance to the law; however, we do not claim the lead of the dark one. I have the will to share more than prior days, so I invest with true leading. I now know God is clearing a path so I will present my knowledge to those who are in need. I believe I may be asked to invite others into the fold and in doing this action may find death has taken me. But to act in accordance with God means fruit is being given. It may be I claim God in a public forum where death will surely be placed upon me. I do not fear as I have the stand of God, but I realize it will not be an easy undertaking. I shake at times and am finding I value Jesus all the more. He never expects me to lie down my life for Him and this is another example of His great way. The enemy of Him does however and I must accept I may soon lose my life. To be scared concerning how this will happen comes to me and then I regain the knowledge to pray is the way to be gifted hope. The strength of the One who holds me fast is far greater than that of man's inflictions. I will always be human till the restoration of my spirit but for now I have human emotions. It is not easy standing knowing I shall have to offer myself in someway, but I do it so others hear the Gospel. This is the plan of God for all to hear His holy way. The intent is for those who receive to gain the favor of Him and to be fed light. I will stand in the way of faith and work so others find this goal for themselves. Belief is vital and in the manner of it faith is built.

The love of man to God holds the heart in the crook of His arm. In the feed of God is the way to find prosperity not hardship. I value the work I have at this time in where I administer to mankind the love of the Father and His Son, Jesus Christ. It is a measure of faith I value above all else. Looking to lean into the knowledge God operates with a clear and ordained way sets my heart afire. I have the unity to support many and, in this understanding, I have learned my heart rewards others in faith. To be as one body in a gathering place has produced hope none compares to. To see others worship the Savior has been a light to me in a personal way. I now realize church is a gift not a loss. I used to enjoy the outing, but I didn't realize the connection of it. I am now working to gift others this value. I stand in the way of knowledge and daily it measures forth to others. I have the trust of God and in knowing Him I find the faith I need to reassure another He is real and good. The prosperity of knowing the Risen God is value to its finest. Seeking Him brings Him close and in the intent stands the sight of unity. God operates where He is invited and to rely on Him for all things good is good character building. I value the way God gifts me support and I now invest the same faith to many. I have the unity that stands with true love, and I believe I am able to conquer the dark by way of His power, not my own but His. I stand in support, and I invite Him to feed me with the Word of His Book of hope. I have compiled many ordained Scriptures and so have many others. We tie them in one booklet and read from the unity with truth. The ability to perfect this unity did not come from my own hand for I am but a being of inspiration from on high. God is the one who made the material not I. I just work as His hands and feet.

5 Your love, O LORD, reaches to the heavens, your faithfulness to the skies. 6 Your righteousness is like the mighty mountains, your justice like the great deep. Psalm 36:5-6 NIV

God, the one who made me complete, stands with character and a witness of faith is put forth. I can withstand the wait in the way of knowing others have found the support from on high. It encourages me deeply and in the way of others finding unity I know it happens as I see the many who have claimed God for themselves. I trust my King is advancing the way ahead with character and I trust in Him for the light bears witness to this. I know I am not without support and in the knowledge, I continue to support another lacking the guidance of Christ. Where there is a blossoming effect, I wait for the manner to claim the need of Him so as to build in the favor of the witness. I do not attempt to make someone learn for this does not happen if force is the bond. It only enhances the negative to be a value in the place of true insight. I have learned many lead and know God as I do. I am seeing others come forth with clear motives to offer others the way just as I am. It is courage bottled in others who enable me to keep pursuing God. Not that alone I wouldn't but the numbers aid my spirit with support while I maintain the trust of the Living God. The teaching I gift is of the same value as Christ for it is by His way I am given the knowledge. The many who believe are building a center with their heart in the way of standing with smiles and eye contact. It is simple; yet, very meaningful. It still remains the only way we can reach out to another without being harnessed to jail. Therefore, I stress its purpose in this moment. I have no other opportunity to lead so I make the step forth with hope knowing I am in the way of following the King. He is the grant provider, and I am His counsel due to Scripture and its light in me. I will not attempt to stand in a righteous way without the knowledge of God speaking through me for there is no better guiding then Christ, the great Waymaker. Today is a sad time for I have heard others have been thrown into the grave due to following the One of hope. I know they are safe now with Christ at their side personally congratulating them on standing strong for Him. Yet, it still bears the heart a pain.

6

To Teach Many is Difficult and Frightening

God is perfect and true, but within me is the stand of Him and it is good. I follow Him with support for He is my mainstay in where I thrive and put forth love. The freedom of knowing where to align my heart is for those who have the faith of a mustard seed. The wavering who fall into the darkness of loss but know a turn away from the ground level of doubt can bring prosperity to the heart. A fleet of ships pursues the many that are attacking the home front. God is the lead in where the captain knows the best maneuver to outwit the enemy. God has the ability to gain mankind the land and sea, so know He is capable of moving your initiative to the pathway of standing that is bright and fulfilling. If you have the wise way about leading, there will come to you a path in where you can thrive and know God is at work on your behalf. Now is the time where mankind has built a damaging way, but the Lord will renew this era and make it vibrant. To love the saving way of Jesus is for man to have the gift of Him within. I operate in where I now have the unity needed to push others in the direction of true hope. I do not advance where I am not welcome as God acts with the same character. To point out the unity I now have is to offer the way to the one seeking to learn. A closed door means no advancement, but if someone is willing to hear for a time a seed gets planted. I know mankind is the one who does not adhere to the Maker of all things good, but when man decides to believe better thought processes are made true. Love is the way to prosperity, so place forward the love of God and be on the plain of a goal leading to wisdom. The path of no insight buries the heart and in the way of it all lose. However, where God is embraced and pursued favor abounds. The mighty way of trust is for the many that have faith God is all-knowing. He is the value man desires to gain a witness to share light and honor. God is the one who has the operating schedule, so know your own unity is based on His directives. He will show you where to gift others with true hope and in doing this act kindness flowers.

To love the One who made the world is to value Him as righteous and true. In His manner comes the offering of faith in where the heart is given the knowing call of the spirit. The unity far surpasses the role of no faith as in the making of the work put forward man derives the plan and is fed to offer hope. I have little in the way of leading due to the dire circumstances before me. God is the one who made my heart and in Him is the love and prosperity needed to thrive. The knowing value is that of Christ the Risen God to all. The way of meeting Him is through prayer and the reading of Scripture. The unity is solid and in it is the light I know resides. I think about the few who have lost their way and realize it was the path they wanted. The darkness is for those who do not desire the King or His better way. Knowing the value of God is a plan many feed to others in where light is abundant. The dark favor is for the person who has no individual way of thinking for they have taken the light and rejected its source. The way to gift unity is for the heart to stand in the unity of God not man. Many feel they have the right to offer a lead of dark due to their understanding they are more valued than another. It is foolish to believe such a lie. God the one who plans the heartbeat and how many there will be within a person is the gateway to life eternal. The lost feel they know all there is to understand; yet, in them is a false unity tied to the enemy of darkness. The way to gain is to provide the spirit with hope from Christ. He is the one who never fails nor loses His demeanor. The sight of God is far more than the witness of one individual. There is a Record in true knowledge that declares many met God in human form. Jesus was this guide of inspiration. The knowing way of unity is in the trust of a person's learning. To value the Scriptures is to know they contain the written truth all man needs to prosper. Favor is for the guiding aspect of knowledge. It is the declaration God is who He claims to be. In Him is the food for bearing forward the light and shining it to another. When we hope to gift others the goal we share from God, a witness flourishes. If you are not in line with care, no value to another is offered. You operate in the way of one who believes he can be fed with a simple knowledge and no authority. Where faith in Christ is embraced, the understanding He is the one all people need to live in glory, and to believe God is the one who created him. The light of knowing the way, to offer others fruit is a goal that builds and aligns with support. Many find they have little to stand on due to the way they carry forward their knowledge. If a bushel of light is granted, it can be a unity to witness from. How does one express hope if he is not adhering to the way of God? In the past, I was not tied to the will of the Waymaker. I had the goal of self with no output to others. I did not think I needed to share any good thing to another. It was a plan of self I played into. Now I see where this was foolishness. I have the reasoning of hope and I plan to gift it to any I am near to. God has gifted me the insight others need to value Him as I do. I now embrace sharing His character and in doing this action I hold the value of Him. Days of insight have flourished, and I have gained a stand of unity that cannot be broken. To believe in the mighty God of all is far better than to reject the gift of insight He has granted.

    The ability to withstand a lean of blank planning is to adhere to light instead. The unity and power of Christ is a gift I gain in the form of favor. I have no hope without the love of God and in Him is my value. The lead of me forward comes into play only due to God and His way of supporting my heart. His leadership is far-reaching, and I know in Him I have the light of faith. God is the one who made me righteous and in His value system I am tied. I am not a formula of labor alone for God supports the person willing to offer unity to others. He will advance you when you offer to another the way of insight. The pathway may not be wealth but rather that of knowing ability to garner to another the scope of Jesus. How will a man gain his value if not supported by Christ? I know I alone cannot make a path of hope. For I am merely flesh and bone with a soul whereas Jesus is spiritual and in Him is the path of beauty none can compare with. I have the faith needed to subscribe another to God, but it is His way of being that draws him to Him. I merely profess the love of God and in doing so share who He is and how to find Him. To work for the benefit of others to have the stand of hope I now hold is character and light. I do not claim to be a miracle worker for God alone is the one who can take a man's idea and make it thrive. He builds with purpose in where the heart learns where to invest and how to know Him. Reading is the latitude of insight forming the goal so believe in the One of great knowledge. Desire Him above all things and find the unity of wisdom within you. God is the one all mankind needs to prosper. It is man who fails to gift others with care. God works within a person to show how to offer a path of knowledge in where beauty is granted in a spiritual way. To have a home of light is to be given the authoring of knowledge that gains you support, and love will grow. Glory is for God the one who made you live. Look toward the One of bright leading and find the faith of a lead that supports your heart and mind. Know God is ever above that of mankind. In the wake of a hope comes the knowledge God is unity and caregiving.

    The One of hope is all one needs to perfect the trust and grow the honor for others to find prosperity. The value of many is for all to realize. God is perfect and in Him is the light of knowing where and when to act. God knows all the angles of the heart and in Him is the pathway of favor. To realize God cares for any who pursue Him in faith is to stand on the character of His way. The vibrant person has the unity and in Him is the gift of support necessary to find the way of truth. People who have no character find the pursuit of Him a waste of time. But one day they will know they chose poorly. It will happen suddenly and in the manner of knowing they have no hope for an eternal gift of life they will charge God with anger thinking to force their agenda. But God knows them from beginning to end and He has the knowledge they would never invite Him in to His way of being. They may try to initiate such a goal but in truth it would be just for the sake of not being cast into a world without light. Many have the unity to realize there is a God, but they do not express Him as the only one of favor. They find they have the ability to withdraw from Him and they choose this as their support. Such deception is within them. Even in death they will not claim God. The one who believes and supports the truth will find life eternal as a gift of hope not death. They will live with purpose and their way will be to pursue God for all time. He will show them where to place their spiritual walk and in the manner of it the light will gain within. God is just. He does not force the walk of Him to another who chooses to leave His presence. He permits them to have their own truth even if it is a lie. Choice means freedom and God granted man the ability to find his own way of thinking. But the one who sees God as holy knows He is all-encompassed and right bearing. To love the One who made you is smart, and trust will blossom. I have never regretted inviting God into me. He has proven to be the stand of light I hold dear. Above all else I claim Jesus for my way of being. In this act I am caring for others who are in need. I align with the support, and I claim God for my own way. I know there is none above Him and He is true love in where all are welcome to find this goal of faith. He supports the many that follow Him and in His way is the gift of truth. He knows all and sees all so none can compare His way to that of others who seem wise but are not for only the King Jesus is all-knowing.

"Father of light, gift us hope so we put you first in our manner of life. Lead us with the guiding way of you and show us where to respond to those in need. I invite your character to my person, and I share your way to others. Thank you for the goal of love and align my character to you. Amen."

I have known my Savior for a period of months; yet, I am fed every drop of hope I need to gift others the value of Him. How does this even happen? By the care and the ministry of the hope I gain in the manner of knowing others find the support needed to know the One of light. I turn to God when I need a vested unity as in Him, I have the trust. Knowing God is for me and all who believe and support Him in faith. It is not I alone am in need for there are many who have searched for Jesus. Those who were willing to gain the recognized unity found the light and proceeded in faith to claim Jesus as

Savior. The One who made me has instructed me with love. I now have the goal of sharing Him in the way of eternal bliss. I know He is the sight plan needed to have life in good standing and there is no greater way than that of Christ to His people. He has the heart of a warrior; yet; He does not fight the one building on His behalf. He operates with character and in Him is the sight of knowing where to gain and how to perform the unity, so others are fed light, too. Do the people who invite Jesus to their person lose identity in Him? Not in the sense of no knowledge of likes and dislikes but the unity is far-reaching in that its value is sacred and right. Glory to God comes forward; yet, God is not one to boast. There is no need for He is far better than all else. I have the gift of sight in where I love the Savior more than my own life. He supports me and I claim Him to my person. In the value of Him I have the knowledge He is gold to me. Far-reaching is His handprint. I watch and look for others who present this knowledge. The form of it is light so an outreach is different from a stand of no fruit. I see a person and if the light is present, they have warmth and honor not a hollow seed within. It can be something as slight as a nod in the corner of the eye in where a twinkle is understood. Light within is a witness to the One of glory. However, many fake this and try to be expressions of good but they are soon recognized as deceivers. I know I could fall victim to one who is not holy driven but as of now God has shown me the people of hope and we have undertaken the leading with character. I walk on from anyone with the mark of death for I know there is no hope for them now. It has taken time to unite in such a way but the will of God to me is standing in support. I now have the talent of a tuned piano and I orchestrate the love to others with care. I do not apply my face on the forefront of the lead, so I wait to see who applies toward me with unity. I have the patience due to Christ who stands with me, and I value this protection with my whole being. I know time may unravel and I may have to offer myself in death to the One of hope. This is not in the way of a sacrificial lamb but that of speaking on behalf of Him. Jesus hung from the tree so I could gain entry to Him, and for this I shall stand for others. I have the unity to Him, and I know I am safe for all time even if death comes I will be secure.

29 The next day John saw Jesus coming toward him and said, "Look, the lamb of God, who takes away the sin of the world! 30 This is the one I meant when I said, 'A man who comes after me has surpassed me because he was before me. 31 I myself did not know him, but the reason I came baptizing with water was that he might be revealed to Israel." John 1:29-31 NIV

I am here as the one to confess the Lord is my hope and no other can match His way. The Word of God is for any who have the staple of Him within. It reaches the heart and in the work of it faith is given. Light is abundant and good in where man finds the benefit of it to his person. The final piece of it comes in the way of leading the spirit to Christ. The way to pursue the love of knowledge is the plant of it within the heart. Reading the Word provides the heart the benefit necessary to abound in freedom. How can this be? It is by the way of the One who made you. He knew what would matter to your makeup. In Him is the value needed to lead and to ordain the heart, so it favors the gift of instruction. Knowing the trust of God is what sets in motion His character to you. When you accept Him for the one of knowledge true garnering occurs. The value of the Waymaker is far above that of any other gift one could gain. How do I know God is true? He has never failed me in all I have given Him. It is the act of worship that draws Him near and in this I learn and guide others to His claim to them. I now hold the value of God due to Him releasing to me His way. It is solid and it never washes my own unity away. I have the knowing ability to offer another who the Witness of love is. In the way of this committed bounty, I have faith. It stands as the glue to Him that is needed to offer another His way. I have taken in His counsel and found it supportive to my heart. It is good and brings forward a role of favor leading me in the direction of Him. His character is right and if I fail to arrive to heaven's door in the way of a silent death I will stand in harmony to God through the criminal action against me. But if I engage in the way of sharing the value of God others will hear and find the truth supports their spirit. I know I am weak, but God is strong, and He is able to support even the slightest investment to Him.

I have the knowing ability to support others who want to learn as I have about Christ and His love of mankind. I now know I am with His spirit and in this knowledge, I have the faith to put into action God is favoring. How shall I continue in the world where I may find myself at a loss for saying truth? I will invest when the pathway is seen as fruitful. In the way of favor, I will gain respect from my Lord and I will act for His glory. I know I am not alone for many have the faith I know due to their own admittance of faith to God. The One who claimed me is far greater then those who speak of governing the people for they think of self over heart unity. Where man finds the faith is due, he works toward the body of it. I now believe I have found the way to life eternal and in doing this I have the heart of God within me. I now see how those before me who were raptured found prosperity. They placed their hearts and minds into the hand of the Living Light known as Jesus. He made them a part of the bride and called them to Him. I would have been raptured too if I invested sooner to the love of Him who came to save me. I now

I am a Scared Witness

have death before me at every turn, but I know I am in the Savior's hands, and nothing can come against me without His permission. He leads me with character of light and in doing so I favor Him with value. The unity far surpasses that of wealth of the pocketbook, so it is Christ-like in its outreach. I have the favor of God and in this I am made righteous. The unity of God is for me to gain by. He is the Crafter, and I am the witness to His perfect way. I thank Him for His way, and I advance with goal making in I strive to know Him with pleasure. He is the one I yearn for. No other is more valuable to me. Does this mean I won't suffer harm? No, for no one knows the way of his livelihood. But the One who developed me stands waiting to reach out and offer me life eternal in where I am safe for all time. He is the one I shall place my hope in for He does not fail to provide. I have His way before me and that is what I choose for my own path of hope. He stands with character and in Him I am fed. Peace comes from His hand.

God, the one who made you, is the value of hope needed to gain a way of thinking. He is the one who divests to the heart where it is to stand and how it should be maintained. The knowing thought process is to follow the One of hope and lead in the same manner. God is sufficient to allow us our own path; but yet, to Him is the way ahead. He is the unity all need to have to obtain the light and grow in the way of sight. Seeing is not the only way to know something is real. Spiritual leading plays a role where man is vested. If you have fallen in love, you know it came to you by the heart and not the physical; but yet, many confuse the two. Have the heart of the One in the stand of gain and allow man to learn from the unity. You do this by reading the Book of love and offering it to others who need the same witness. God supports the one who has the way of favor. How this happens is where many find the faith and divest it to others who too, do the same action. God supports the many that have the guiding of Him to their person. In the way of faith man is fed the unity of God and a witness is offered. The faith of mankind is not resting in man's hands. God has the timing of the unity and in Him is the faith of the many who have invested in Him with trust. God knows who cares for others and who is at work to destroy them. The dark one does not value any person or thing. A dog handler can be a person of hope but if he does not have Christ as his personal Savior he is merely pretending to place value on the animal. That is where the light comes into play. The way of a committed person will be to offer the gift in a free manner without the brand of a sales pitch. Yes, ministry needs to be fed in cash flow, but when in casual conversation no fee should be applied. Even when a person acknowledges another true hope can build. Character is standing for others, so none perish. If a person is outright against his fellowman, there is no light within him. He only caters to the one who has the same inherit stand as he does, he is not gifting unity. He merely stands with the one who is with him as far as friendship goes. This can mean many you know may not have the goal of unification. God needs to be the one you bind your heart toward. He is the Crafter of light and in Him is the unity necessary to push the knowledge forward and carry it to the heart of all. Leading is the way to find true hope as it stands as a witness to many in need. I have the inherit thought process I can build where another needs to find support. This is an act of insight as God gave me the knowledge of how to offer this gain. He alone made all man into His image so all can bear witness to Him. Seek the way of God and be standing with support leading to character and a measure of faith will be forthcoming.

God is the perfect way to thrive and find the faith of the knowing lead all need to nourish their hearts and minds. God is the unity to offer where others have the benefit of knowing the Savior and in this way can operate with character. Why does this mean a gain? I have the willing heart of faith and in the maintenance of it I am given the support of knowing God is perfect and true. To know this is to offer the faith to another who is in need. I have declared this knowledge; and yet, I am not able to speak publicly for fear of death. I would have spoken to the care of God in the way of favor before had I known I would be in this time frame. I stood without the love of man and in the way of no faith I did not offer the light as it was not within me. I thought I had the lead but in truth I had none. Though I did not go against the One of hope I did not support Him in the way of faith. I did not tell others of Him, and I did not invite Him within me. I knew I rejected the offered gain; and yet, I did not accept this as truth. Why was I so without hope? I thought I had knowledge of time. I did not believe I would stand in front of God before I was old and weathered. However, here I am; a person of youth with no intent to neither marry nor can I speak of such things for we are not permitted this luxury. I now must offer all the idea of the governing body if I am to be standing with them or I will be made to stand in the guard and hung from the rafters. I do not dream of any yielded way other than that of Jesus and His manner. I must accept I am forever to be without children as they are not permitted either. They are thought of as a burden on society, so no one has the nerve to carry out the full-term pregnancy. It is a small thing for man to have the intention of harming others for it happens readily due to no favor in the way of truth. Only the ones who understand God is the way offer no intent to harm. This makes it difficult to thrive and work for fear of violence in the work field. I have the way of pretending to offer a lead in where I graft to the falseness, but I do not really do so. The dark one does not hold value and in his way that is all that exists. I now know there is no hope for any which have the mark and I would be in such a stand had I not understood the call of God to me. I took the light and asked for truth in where God provided it to me. He was the one who gave me the way to learn and to hear so I am more than pleased to share Him where able. The knowing people work in the quiet and lean into one another in character. We do not set a sight of leading where others see until such a time presents. I have the work of a knowing individual and in the way of favor God has supported me. I do not enjoy simple witnesses from the enemy even though it means life as far as the physical so I do not obtain the material he puts forth. It is in direct conflict to the One who made me, and it goes against my heart.

22 Who is the liar? It is the man who denies that Jesus is the Christ. Such a man is the antichrist-he denies the Father and the Son. 1 John 2:22 NIV

The leading of the One who never fails is not that of no-unity. He is far better than the way of the deceptive player known as Satan. For this entity is false and bears no truth. In Satan alone is the way of death for that is all he is made of. God did not make this, but he chose the path for himself. He was to be a bright being of hope in the form of an angel. There resides no gift of hope for he is all darkness. No light carries forward from him. Many have the thought process money can be light, but they are fooled, and Satan is the one doing the lead. He is not value for he is all death leading to a loss that cannot change. The more a person invests in the darkness the less draw the Father has. It is a dark way of being and in it is the material lead of no hope. God is the one who made mankind. He made him with character; yet, knowing some would desire a different unity he allowed for him to choose his own way. I have no offering of hope without Christ nor does any who have ever lived. The many who have gone on before me now know the truth of who was the better way. Whether they believed or did not there is only life of faith or death. Those are the only two options. So, stand in the way of clear gain and believe with hope so as to have the inheritance of Christ. The guiding influence of Jesus is that of faith and light. You can know the difference by asking God to show you the truth of the life of Him. He will not fail you if you profess with love and character to Him. The One of light does not fail to justify His own stand so know in Him is the way for gain. I am tied to Him for all time and thankful to be so.

Unity is for the man who has the faith of knowing God is character and harmony to the heart. Where the favor comes into play is the manner of truth being given, the One who dreams for mankind to have Him as their manner is the guide for all to have within. The counselor is the Holy Spirit and in Him is the knowing ability to pave the plan to the spirit. The insight does not leave the believer. It is always present and always right and good. The acceptance of such a gift happens when one professes the Savior as his Lord. To know the King in a personal way is to align with Him to teach and to lead others. The two are unity in Him. He permits man to take up the cross of bearing fruit to many in the way of sharing the witness of gain. I now realize I could have been one to lead had I believed before now, but I can't change the fact I did not. I have now the hope to offer many the fact God is true and good and in doing this knowledge others will adhere to the Savior as I have. The work of God is for any to have Him as their witness at the time of judgment. He is the one who makes the gateway for man to have eternal gain in Him. Love is what makes Him stand on man's behalf. The way of trust is built by Him so know when you pray forward the Word of God comes forth.

26 But the Counselor, the Holy Spirit, whom the Father will send in my name, will teach you all things and will remind you of everything I have said to you. John 14:26 NIV

God is the character of man leading to favor and hope. In the way of faith man is not one to undervalue the righteous way if he has the knowledge of the One who made him. The one who offers the light to others is seeing clearly how to operate in where hope is gifted. I have the knowing of a soldier in where I fight to share the Gospel in a time of little light. The need is real, and the converts are not readily found. However, I know I am not one to be shy if God has shown me where to offer Him to another. I work as though I am part of a team of the lost, when in actuality, I know the One who made all things good. I do not profess to doubt, but rather I remain quiet as if to have no understanding. In the event I am to gain more of an outreach by saying aloud the name of Jesus I will support my God in this way. For now, I am not inspired to act in such a manner. I believe I have the gift of hope due to the many who have prayed for my welfare. God is dutiful and in Him is the knowledge of mankind. The way of Christ is to share the Gospel and put it in motion. I know authors from the past have had the vision of leading many to the love of the Risen King. Many have found the support, and their material is present in the heart of man. I look where I can for such garnering, but it is far from visible. I have understood some write today in secret and post it forward by way of no name being applied. They do not sign the work nor do you know where to find the one who wrote the work. God is making a play for man even in the way of no limelight. Reading is a gift, so we are banned from this too. However, many do engage in the practice, and they witness a growing hope as a result. God leads me to share what I know and in doing this action others have the light of my experiences. God is the goal for me to align to. I have the knowing sight of care as a result. I lead so another can have the unity I know is gained. I love the lead of God and in the way of His favor I am fed truth. I know others also understand how to find the truth of the Word for there have been notes attached to my heart by way of a joint prayer in the spirit. I have heard others pray for my welfare and for my continued outreach to be secure. I do not squander this unity and in the way of others I pray, too. Knowing the way to profess light is a gift of hope. The trust is what others find as well when they have the knowledge of God within them. I know I am not the only person to witness as others have shared their connection. We offer light to one another, and we believe our hearts are wired to hear the voice of truth as one body. I do not see how we would be able to perform the conversations we have outside of this unity. Today, all are required to stand on behalf of the evil one. I do not intend to lay forth my favor to him so soon I will be put forward as a traitor. I know I have little time to voice the heart of God to others, so I bend to God just as I am. He knows where to place me for the best advantage and in the object of His care I am safe. I see the role of author before me. Not as one who writes but one who administers to fellow people who are searching just as I used to be. I can clearly hear their frustration in trying to gain the light. I pray and aid in this way knowing God hears me and He will honor my words to Him.

God is light and in Him is the way to offer another bounty leading to life eternal. I have the will of knowing I am not without the love of Him due to the way He guides my heart. I stand in unity and with clear insight with character and hope. God is the way to know the lead of support necessary to gain one a factor of faith. Due to my reading of Scripture, I learn the way to stand as an honorary bride member. Who is the light for? It is for all who have the way of God within them. Every single person can rest in the arms of the Savior but not all choose Him as they like the dark one better. It seems so hard to imagine someone who accepts the dark way over the light, but it is true. Wherever man finds faith comes the respect of God and in this measure is the eternal hope. The Living Word is alive, and it maintains the spirit as to what is valued and what is not right or good. I know I have been given the sight of care and in this form, I now have faith. I read the truth due to the way it guides me and how it offers me the path of goodness. I enjoy applying the witness I have and in doing so others, too, have the benefit of eternal light. The revelation God is the being of goodness laid claim to my heart and made it justified. To look to the One of good harmony is to invite Him forth for the gain to my heart. No light comes without Jesus being the one to grant it. He will not claim someone who does not call to Him and ask for forgiveness. If you desire to have the favor of God and you do not willingly put away a sinful lifestyle there is no authoring within you. Every believer has committed sin. Sin resides within us but how we approach it is what makes the difference. If we practice sin as a lifestyle, we have rejected God and chosen it over the love of the One who made us. I have no doubt I am not perfect, but I know I have conquered sin in many areas of my way of being. I do not have all the light of the Caregiver of man, but I shall not feed a black way of being. If something compels me to act out of character and to entertain it due to support above the unity of the Most High, I do not engage. I have no offered control if the rejection is constant. I have the witness of knowing there are many who have the gift of seeing where I have fallen and in this; I do not wish to portray the loss. I have determined the path of sin is something I will not partake of. It takes the will of God for the unity to be standing and I embrace Him with the true nature of His way. The battle may be hard but the way to thrive is to stand in the knowledge God is far stronger than sin nature. I have overcome much with the acquisition of the Word to my heart. I know I am not always going to act with total gain, but I will not succumb to a loss if I am dedicated to the light.

God's work is not all the way to have hope, but it is for the one who cares about his fellowman. God's work is to grant others the way of Him to their hearts and minds. To pray is to offer others the plan of unity and guide them with character. The One who made mankind supports the individual who has the heart of the Author within him. The will and care supporting the way of Christ comes into play when a person believes and invites the unity. God has the trust and in Him is the way to prepare the steadfast bond of faith. I believe man is not all-knowing and I understand God fills that role. Due to the realization God is perfect I am here to testify God never fails. By His commitment to mankind, we have the plan of salvation granted to our hearts. I know it took time for God to draw me forward to Him but now I am standing in favor of His name. He is my all in all. I have the trust of Him and in this unity, I am fed light. How can this element stand in the region of today? God is not one to lose His stamina or His manner. No force can come against Him and win. In the end Satan will be cast into the lake of fire to never harm mankind again. The witness of this is found in Scripture.

> ***10 And the devil, who deceived them, was thrown into the lake of burning sulfur, where the beast and false prophet had been thrown. They will be tormented day and night forever and ever. Revelation 20:10 NIV***

God shall never fail, nor will He lose His way of being. He stands in support of all who have the faith within to support Him with character. The way of faith is for mankind to unite in wise leading and to offer another the path of fruit. I shall proclaim this forward till death; and in the witness, others will hear the light spread. I am closing with the knowledge God has me safe and He will never lead me astray.

5 Into your hands I commit my spirit; redeem me, O LORD, the God of truth. Psalm 31:5 NIV

Robin (Rochel) Arne

Author Bio

Robin Arne is dedicated to the role of sharing the hope to others who need to hear the truth of the Word. God cares about her strategy in writing, and He favors her with the will of His hand. The witness is for all to learn and gain. It is her lifestyle to stand on behalf of the many who have found her writings and to tell the witness of grace. God is true in His demeanor, and He offers the light of Him to Robin's pen. Her daily work is to hear the Scripture words and to have the faith it takes to lead others for the sake of Christ. She is not alone, and many others have this same drive. She has learned she stands with the bride of God and in doing so her heart engages with unity. She now has the knowing ability to offer light and unity. God has shown her where to place her heart and it is with Him in the way of professing the faith of God to all. The plan to share God is all that inspires Robin. She works both in clay and with writing, so she has many forms of outreach. Today, she has the honor of hearing the Lord speak and this is a gift she claims is righteous. The unity is a sight of birth she invests in. Scripture is the lead of faith she gains and, in the reading, comes the vision of support. Her heart is faith bearing; so she stands in the wait for others to learn as she has.

advbookstore.com

Robin (Rochel) Arne